PROFESSIONAL
BARTENDING

PROFESSIONAL BARTENDING

Adam W Freeth

NEW HOLLAND

First published in 2009 by New Holland Publishers (UK) Ltd
London • Cape Town • Sydney • Auckland

Garfield House
86–88 Edgware Road
London W2 2EA
United Kingdom
www.newhollandpublishers.com

80 McKenzie Street
Cape Town 8001
South Africa

Unit 1
66 Gibbes Street
Chatswood
NSW 2067
Australia

218 Lake Road
Northcote
Auckland
New Zealand

ISBN 978 1 84773 055 8

Senior Editor: Corinne Masciocchi
Designer: Peter Crump
Photographer: Edward Allwright
Production: Marion Storz
Editorial Direction: Rosemary Wilkinson

2 4 6 8 10 9 7 5 3 1

Reproduction by PDQ Digital Media Solutions Ltd, UK
Printed and bound by Craft Print International Ltd, Singapore

Contents

Introduction 6

THE PROFESSIONAL BARTENDER 8

RESPONSIBLE SERVICE OF ALCOHOL 14

THE CUSTOMER 16

THE BAR ENVIRONMENT 24

PRODUCT KNOWLEDGE 52

Grain distillates: Vodka 58

Grain distillates: Gin 61

Grain distillates: Whisky 64

Plant distillates: Rum 71

Plant distillates: Cachaça 75

Plant distillates: Tequila and Mezcal 76

Fruit distillates: Brandy 79

Aromatised/Fortified Wines 82

Bitters 83

Liqueurs 84

Wine and Champagne 87

Beers 91

THE MECHANICS OF BARTENDING 94

COCKTAILS AND MIXOLOGY 102

COCKTAIL RECIPES 108

Acknowledgements 158

Index 158

Introduction

Bartending dates back to ancient times and can be found in Roman, Greek and even Asian societies. Then, as now, public drinking houses or inns served as a meeting place for people to socialise with their friends over a couple of drinks.

It was not until the early 19th century that the first cocktail was invented, marking the beginning of a new era in bartending. Shortly afterwards, in 1862, the first cocktail recipe book was published. Written by an American bartender named Jerry Thomas, *The Bartender's Guide: How to Mix Drinks*, introduced the art of cocktail making to a wider audience. Though he did not invent the cocktail per se, Thomas is considered the Father of the cocktail, promoting them with his travelling cocktail show, and concocting his famous Blue Blazer with a display of theatre and showmanship – displaying the kind of skills that we still see in bars around the world today. A second cocktail book followed shortly afterwards. In 1888 Harry Johnson published the *New and Improved Bartender's Manual of How to Mix Drinks*. Johnson is noted to have tended bar in Chicago, Boston and New York from around the 1860s.

Over the last couple of centuries, many notable bartenders – too many to mention – have left their lasting mark in bartending history and have contributed to the progression and recognition of professional bartending the world over. Though the style of bartending has evolved since its early beginnings, the concept has very much remained the same.

The hospitality industry has experienced a flourish in the last few decades and never have experienced, professional bartenders been more in demand. It is with this in mind that the idea for this book was hatched. Covering all aspects of bartending, from getting to grips with the inner workings of a bar, understanding the products you are selling, alcohol awareness, recipe development and dealing with the public in an efficient and professional manner, this guide will reveal the ins and outs of how to run a modern-day bar. So whether you're looking to improve your own skills or wishing to make a profession out of bartending, this book provides all the advice and answers you need.

THE PROFESSIONAL BARTENDER

THE PROFESSIONAL BARTENDER

When exploring what defines a professional bartender, one must first look at what 'professional' means in the context of bartending. The word 'professional' is defined in many ways to mean much the same thing, one that is skilful by virtue of possessing special knowledge or a person having impressive competence in a particular skill.

As a result, today's bartenders are expected to keep up with the ever-changing pace of global hospitality and service standards. Professional bartenders must now be more knowledgeable, quicker, more efficient, friendlier and more focused on keeping the customer delighted than ever before.

THE FIVE PS

The five Ps represent all that encompasses a professional bartender:
Pride, Passion, Preparation, Presentation, Professionalism.

A professional bartender will always exude enthusiasm and passion for their profession; they will take pride in how they look and what they do behind the bar. Preparation and presentation are just as important to them as any top chef. Just like a professional chef, a professional bartender will have a keen eye for detail and have a plethora of classic recipes that they have perfected whilst having the creativity and knowledge of ingredients to invent their very own concoctions.

Although not a technical skill, style is vital to the modern bartender. It can be represented in many different ways and, remembering that over 70 per cent of communication is non-verbal, here are a few pointers to consider:
• **Personality:** use your personality to develop your style
• **Confidence:** comes with knowledge and practice
• **Pours:** the style in which you pour, accurately and with panache
• **Shake:** unique and with presence. It's an art form so enjoy it!
• **Showmanship:** presentation of practical and flair skills
• **Presentation:** your own personal style, adapted to the environment.

This book aims to provide the novice and aspiring bartender with the practical know-how to become a professional bartender. No one book can singularly provide all the skills and knowledge necessary to become a proficient, efficient and accomplished bartender but, with lots of practical experience and training, this book will help you get one step closer to being a professional bartender.

JOB DESCRIPTION

As a professional bartender your job is not only to provide efficient and friendly service, but to use your extensive knowledge of the bar menu to suggest and sell appropriate drinks to fulfil your guests' needs. Furthermore, it is your responsibility to produce all liquid refreshments and to ensure that the bar is maintained to the highest standards of cleanliness and presentation.

Job-specific requirements and responsibilities:
• **Punctuality:** be on time, every time. Punctuality is vital in the bar arena; it is a true sign of the professional and ranks very highly with all operators/managers. Lateness affects everyone around you as all operations work as a team.
• **Personal appearance:** every bar, restaurant, hotel, nightclub, casino

and café will have its own policy on uniform and appearance. Everyone should look professional and no matter what environment you are working in you should take pride in your appearance and personal hygiene. Close contact with customers and team members means that deodorant is a prerequisite. Fingernails and hair should be kept clean at all times and if your hair is long, tie it back.

• **Uniform:** your uniform is either issued or set as a standard by the venue. Be sure to keep your uniform clean and ironed, and your shoes polished. Always remember that you are an ambassador for your bar and bartenders.

Personal bar tools

As a minimum, bartenders should always carry three pens on their person (one to use, one to lose and one to give away), a lighter and a waiter's friend. Professional bartenders will also have their own bartending kit, which can include a Boston shaker, strainers, bar blades, pour spouts, bar spoons, a muddler, a canelle knife, a chopping knife and board, and many other tools.

Attitude

A positive attitude is vital in the hospitality industry and as a bartender you are constantly in contact with people, customers or team members. There is no room for arrogance or negativity and your attitude should be positive whenever on duty. Smile and mean it or change jobs.

Preparation

Similarly to a kitchen, a bar requires a lot of preparation to ensure the smooth running of a shift. All service areas and stations should be set up to the venue's standard and should be 100 per cent ready for business at opening time. Till floats, change, glassware, garnishes, ice, napkins, straws and stock should all be checked and plentiful. Your responsibility is to complete all bar set-ups, along with operational and breakdown duties set out by your venue's standards.

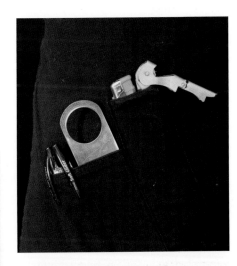

customers. Your job is to serve alcohol but this must be done responsibly with both your customers' and your staff's safety in mind. See pages 14–15 for further information.

Customer service

Good customer service is not just about serving guests drinks with a smile. Your responsibility as a bartender is to ensure that every stage of the service process is performed to the highest possible standards and to ensure your guests leave feeling delighted about their impression of you and experience of your service.

Multi-tasking

You should always endeavour to use both hands whenever possible; multi-tasking involves doing more than one thing at a time. There are many small jobs that need doing throughout a bar shift aside from making drinks, including clearing away dirty glassware, restocking, replenishing ice, napkins and straws, checking back to customers, standing menus up, placing a fresh napkin under a customer's drink and, of course, cleaning the bar. A bartender should always aim to stay on top of these tasks, some of which can be done simultaneously, such as replenishing straws whilst checking back to the customer or taking an order whilst placing a fresh napkin under a customer's drink.

Teamwork

Teamwork is an essential part of running a bar and the success of many. Your job as a professional bartender is to support your team members and always be a team player. There is a saying in the industry that goes: 'if you are not serving, serve your team mates'.

Service is all-important. When a large group of people enters your bar, if you are not serving a customer, stop what you are doing and split the order with your colleagues. Do not be afraid to ask others for help – they will soon ask you when they need it. Alternatively, be alert and attentive to your colleagues' needs; teamwork can be as small as passing a bottle, placing napkins and making drinks in your colleague's order, icing their glassware or simply cleaning and clearing their service area. Interaction and communication are the key to effective teamwork.

Licensing laws and regulations

All laws and regulations governing the sale of alcohol on licensed premises vary around the world, so it is important that you are familiar with your country's and venue's rules. For instance, in the UK and Australia it is illegal to serve alcohol to anyone under the age of 18; in the US the limit varies between 18 and 21 years old. It is your own personal responsibility to know the local laws on serving alcohol. The responsible service of alcohol also extends to intoxication and in some cases fines may be issued for serving individuals who may be intoxicated.

Serving alcohol responsibly

Serving someone who may appear drunk can be bad for business, and can endanger the customers and/or staff. Your role is prevention rather than cure and you should, whenever possible, monitor the alcohol intake of your

Money handling

Any money that is handled within the bar environment should always be checked carefully and accurately at all times. Bartenders work in a fast-paced, noisy and energetic environment so it's important to be vigilant and focused on the money. In most cases venue managers hold responsible the individual bartenders or those who have shared a cash register for any discrepancies, either negative or positive. Always count change back either into the customer's hand or onto a change tray, with a receipt where possible.

> **BARTENDER'S TIP:** Always call out to the customer any note that is handed to you, for example, 'That's a twenty'. This will ensure that there are no discrepancies. This can help as a reminder of the note you are tendering to avoid accidentally short-changing a customer. It makes the customer clear on the note they handed over and avoids them thinking that they may have been short-changed.

Cleanliness

Cleaning is a large part of a bartender's job: cleaning bar tops, service areas, washing out shakers and tools, and clearing away dirty glasses are some of the many cleaning jobs. Professional bartenders should maintain the highest standards of bar cleanliness and hygiene at all times, before, during and after their shift. Keeping the bar spotless is a sign of a great bartender. A clean and tidy bar top is inviting to the guests so clean as you go (CAYG). Equipment and glassware should also be kept clean and shining at all times, particularly shakers and mixing glasses.

Health and safety

Bartenders have a personal responsibility to work safely and without risk to others by adhering to company industry health and safety procedures. Remember that you are handling foodstuff and liquid for consumption, so cleanliness of preparation and storage are of the utmost importance. If mopping any floor area, always be sure to display any appropriate warning signs.

Company policies

Be aware of all company licensing laws, policies and procedures. Each bar will have their own procedures, policies and laws, and it is your job to learn these before you set foot behind the bar.

Reporting

Bartenders should assist the management in maintaining and exceeding standards by reporting any problems with the bar and working environment. If a customer has cause for complaint and would like to speak to a manager, unless it is something that you are confident and comfortable handling, ensure you report this to a manager or supervisor immediately.

Knowledge

You must have a full knowledge of all products and prices within your operation. Your knowledge is only limited to your willingness to learn and educate yourself and absorb the experience from the bars you work in.

Education

To actively contribute to your business, you should strive to improve yourself and the business you work for by continually learning and educating yourself about your chosen profession.

RESPONSIBLE SERVICE OF ALCOHOL

Although most people drink alcohol responsibly, alcohol abuse by a small minority can result in crime, health risks and anti-social behaviour. The professional bartender can play a vital role in the responsible service and promotion of alcohol, and must be aware of any local laws and regulations that govern its sale and consumption.

INTOXICATION

Intoxication can have a dramatic effect on a person's behaviour, and bartenders have a responsibility to be proactive in the prevention of persons becoming unduly intoxicated and to ensure the safety of all customers. In some countries it is illegal to knowingly sell alcohol to a person who is drunk or appears drunk. Equally it is an offence to serve alcohol to the companion of a person who is drunk for the drunken person's consumption.

Common signs of intoxication:
- Slurring and mispronunciation
- Staggering, swaying or clumsiness
- Looking sleepy (eyes rolling back)
- A significant change in behaviour as well as anti-social behaviour
- Speaking loudly and the inability to hear properly

DRINK DRIVING

Bartenders should always have their clients' safety in mind when selling or serving drinks. If you are aware that any of your clientele is driving, always be in a position to offer an alternative non-alcoholic beverage.

UNDER-AGE DRINKING

In some countries serving alcohol to minors is illegal and bartenders can face personal fines and criminal charges. Ensure you check the local licensing laws and regulations. Bartenders should always be prepared to ask a customer for proof of age. Be sensitive in your approach to any customer that may appear under the legal drinking age so as not to cause unnecessary embarrassment.

WHAT HAPPENS TO ALCOHOL IN YOUR BODY?

The alcohol in drink is absorbed into your body through the stomach and small intestine. Food slows down the rate of absorption – that's why alcohol affects you more quickly on an empty stomach.

From here, it is distributed via the bloodstream throughout the body, reaching your heart, brain, muscles and other tissues. This happens very quickly – within a few minutes. Usually, though not always, this has a pleasant effect.

Your body can't store alcohol, so it has to get rid of it, mostly via your liver. First, the liver changes alcohol into a highly toxic substance called acetaldehyde. This turns into acetate, a harmless substance, which is passed out in the urine. Some alcohol is also excreted through the breath and sweat. Your body's ability to process alcohol depends on various factors like your age, weight and sex. Your body breaks down alcohol at a rate of about one unit per hour – and no, there is no way you can speed this up!

ALCOHOL AND UNIT MEASUREMENT

Everyone involved in the sale of alcohol should be aware of the strengths of drinks they serve and should be prepared to give customers informed advice. The panel opposite illustrates how to measure a unit of alcohol and the effects of alcohol on the body.

Some customers may wish to know the levels of alcohol contained in different drinks to monitor their alcohol intake. So that this may be done, a measurement called a 'unit of alcohol' is used, one unit equating to 8 g or 10 ml of alcohol.

Half a pint of beer, at a strength of 3.5% ABV, contains 8 g of alcohol, or 1 unit (or to be specific 1.0255 units). One 25 ml jigger of vodka, at a strength 40% ABV, also contains 8 g alcohol. Therefore, in terms of alcohol intake, one jigger of vodka is equivalent to half a pint of beer.

ALCOHOL AND THE BODY

Alcohol is absorbed into the blood and reaches all parts of the body, and the effect drinking has on an individual depends on how much alcohol is in the bloodstream at any given time, in other words, the blood alcohol concentration (BAC).

The amount of alcohol that gets into the bloodstream and how quickly depends on quantity, gender, build and ingested food. All these factors combined make an accurate diagnosis of a person's BAC almost impossible.

Other important factors affecting BAC:
Volume: the amount of alcohol consumed and the strength (ABV% or proof).
Size and weight: if you are small, your blood alcohol volume is less than that of a larger person.
Sex: women can't drink as much as men – it's a biological fact! Women are generally smaller and have proportionately less body water and more body fat than men, and alcohol doesn't dissolve easily in fat. That's

Vodka: 25 ml at 40% ABV = 1 unit
Beer: 275 ml at 5% ABV = 1.375 units
Wine: 175 ml at 12.5% ABV = 2.18 units

The number of units of alcohol in any quantity of any drink can be worked out by applying the following formula: **Amount of liquid in ml x % ABV x 0.001.** Here are some common examples:

• Single measure (25 ml) of Smirnoff vodka at 40% ABV = 1 unit

• Standard measure (50 ml) of Graham's port at 20% ABV = 1 unit

• Half a pint (284 ml) of Heineken beer at 5% ABV = 1.42 units

• Small glass (125 ml) of Moët & Chandon Brut Imperial NV at 12% ABV = 1.5 units

• Bottle (275 ml) of Smirnoff Ice at 5.5% ABV = 1.5 units

• Small glass (125 ml) of wine at 12% ABV = 1.5 units

• Double measure (50 ml) of Jack Daniel's whiskey at 40% ABV = 2 units

• Medium glass (175 ml) of wine at 12% ABV = 2 units

• One pint (568 ml) of Guinness stout at 4.1% ABV = 2.4 units

• One pint (568 ml) of Stella Artois lager at 5.2% ABV = 2.95 units

• Large glass (250 ml) of wine at 12% ABV = 3 units

• Double measure of La Fée absinthe at 68% ABV = 3.4 units

why, drink for drink, women end up with more alcohol in their bloodstream than men.
Water level: if you're dehydrated, alcohol will have a greater effect than if your body's water concentration is normal. That's why drinking alcohol in summer or after exercise affects you more.
Ingested food: if you drink a unit of alcohol on an empty stomach, almost all of it will be absorbed in an hour. But if there's food in your stomach, the process will be slower.

The sole cause of drunkenness is drinking alcohol at a rate faster than your body can process it. Usually, about 20 minutes after the last drink, BAC starts to fall. Some alcohol is lost through the lungs and some is lost through urine but most is removed by the liver as blood circulates through it.

BAC levels and their effects on the body	
BAC (mg/ decilitre)	Symptoms
50	Euphoria, talkativeness, relaxation
100	Central nervous system depression, impaired motor and sensory functions, impaired cognition
140	Decreased blood flow to brain
300	Stupefaction, possible unconsciousness
400	Possible death
550	Death highly likely

THE CUSTOMER

THE CUSTOMER

The success of your establishment relies on repeat business, which in turn relies on customer satisfaction. Treat your customers with courtesy and respect and they will not only come back but will pass on the good word to others.

READING YOUR CLIENTELE

The more time spent behind the bar, the more experience you will gain in dealing with people and the better you will be able to anticipate their wants and needs. Reading your clientele takes some sensitivity and a whole lot of common sense. Always be attentive to people's likes and dislikes. A slightly older/more sophisticated group or business customers may prefer to opt for a more refined drink selection rather than a Sex on the Beach cocktail. This is not to say that they may not enjoy or order this drink but bear in mind that this type of drink may be best suited to a hen party or a group of young females. Without generalising too much, reading your clientele is about understanding key groups of people.

Taking into consideration the points raised above, age and popularity may play a role in the type of drinks you suggest to your customers. Suggesting a classic martini to a young couple or student may not be the most suitable recommendation as certain drinks will appeal to different ages, sexes, groups and events.

One the most important points to remember is that the clientele must always be at the heart of your operation. Customer satisfaction is far more important than increasing your overall take on the bar. Unless the clientele leaves your bar planning to make a return visit, the size of their bill will be completely irrelevant. Your business will only survive on repeat business. You must understand this before you even attempt to sell or serve a drink.

CUSTOMER SERVICE

Customer service is often seen as a process, activity, performance measurement and a philosophy. There are hundreds of definitions of customer service; companies and individuals will have their own definition and some bars will have their own customer service standards.

Customer service is a process of how successfully an organisation is able to consistently and repeatedly exceed the needs and expectations of their customers. By and large it is about treating others as you would like to be treated yourself.

One of the things that sets apart someone simply who works behind a bar to a professional bartender is the ability to exceed the needs of the customer. People have the choice to drink and socialise wherever they choose, and even when serving the simplest of drinks that requires very little skill, such as a beer, the standards of service can vary hugely depending on the individual bartender. Using the example below, here are two bartenders serving the same drink to the same customer in the same environment and under the same circumstances.

Bartender A: Someone who works behind a bar
- Customer approaches the bar.
- Bartender looks at the customer, no smile, no words.
- Customer asks for a bottle of beer.
- Bartender takes the first bottle of house beer from the fridge and places the beer in front of the customer, then holds out his hand for payment.
- Customer hands the bartender a note.
- Bartender tenders the note and gives the customer the change.

Bartender B: A professional bartender
- Customer approaches the bar.
- Bartender acknowledges the customer, whilst wiping down the bar and placing a napkin in front of him. The bartender greets the customer and asks what they would like.

- Customer asks for a bottle of beer.
- Bartender suggests a range of beers.
- Customer asks for one of the suggested beers.
- Bartender commends the customer for their choice and asks if they'd like a glass for the beer.
- Customer says 'yes please'.
- Bartender asks the customer if they would like anything else.
- Customer says 'no thanks'.
- Bartender takes a cold bottle of beer from the fridge and presents the label to the customer for approval and provides a clean glass.
- Bartender tells the customer how much it will be.
- Customer hands the bartender a note.
- Bartender calls out the note, tenders it and gives the customer the change.
- Bartender completes the order by thanking the customer.

It may seem that Bartender B does three times as much and takes much longer to serve the customer than Bartender A, but apart from the few seconds of interaction with the customer the service takes the same time but has a much more positive impact on the customer's experience.

The quality of a service experience determines both customer satisfaction or dissatisfaction and the likelihood of a return visit. It is extremely important that when you serve a customer you deliver a service of impeccable standards. Have a passion about what you do; if you are having a good time at work,

then your guests will also have fun. Leave your problems behind when you get behind the bar – it will come across to the guests you are serving.

THE CUSTOMER JOURNEY

Almost 30 per cent of customers will not return to an establishment as a result of poor service received from the person serving them or dissatisfaction felt for the product they have been served.

It could be said that a good bartender does not sell drinks but rather satisfaction to a wide range of needs. As a bartender, customer satisfaction should always be at the centre of what you do. With this in

mind the licensed retail industry is a service industry and all who work behind a bar must understand this. Use the following customer journey as a guide to ensure that your guests receive superior service from the moment they enter your bar to the moment they leave.

The smile
When a customer enters a bar the last thing they want is a miserable bartender to grunt at them after they have just finished a hard day at the office. First impressions always last and this begins with a simple smile and positive eye contact.

The welcome

Try to greet each new customer within 20 to 30 seconds of them entering the venue and don't just focus on the ones you are serving. This is one of the most important processes of the customer journey. If you are cleaning glasses, stocking fridges, sorting change or making a drink you should always acknowledge any new customers to the bar. This can be in the form of a nod, a simple greeting or a courteous 'I'll be with you in just a moment'. By acknowledging your guest you are telling them that you know they are there. This gives them reassurance, especially when the bar is busy, and they will be more inclined to wait. Welcoming a guest into your bar is a vital part of the service process and will immediately make them feel at home and at ease in the bar environment.

The acknowledgement

If you are four-deep with customers, then try to just acknowledge or say 'I'll be with you in a moment'. Even if you are busy, try to give a waiting guest a drinks menu if they haven't already lunged for one. When you are ready to serve a new guest/group, place a napkin in front of the guest or more appropriately a number of napkins for the size of the group.

The use of napkins or drinks coasters are also a good way of letting other bartenders know who is being served. A napkin placed in front of a guest alerts your colleagues that the customer is being served; no napkin means the customer is waiting to be served. For this system to operate properly everyone you work with should know this rule and ensure that once the guests have been served the napkins are cleared from the bar.

The order

When taking an order always be polite and make sure you get the whole order by asking the guest if they would like anything else; it will save you a lot of time. Use expressions such as 'Can I get you anything else?' or 'Is that everything?'.

The sale

This is your sales opportunity, an opening to up-sell or suggest an

appropriate drink. Some bartenders simply take orders, professional bartenders offer service that sells.

The making

Always try to prepare the drink in front of the customer. There aren't many environments where the end product can be influenced so greatly by the person it is served by. Whether it's pouring a beer or making a Manhattan, every drink should be served efficiently and to the highest possible standards, taking into consideration factors such as temperature, presentation, glassware, garnish and much more besides. Try to make the drinks in a rational way by building an order gradually; larger orders can be broken down into twos, threes or

fours. Also break down orders that require different methods. For instance, in the following round of drinks, you would deal with them by order of complexity, starting with the easiest first:

2 bottled beers → open the bottled beers

1 glass of wine → pour the wine

2 Vodka and Cranberry and 1 Cosmopolitan → make these two drinks together

Style and entertainment

Because of your personality, your style of service will probably be different to the next bartender. Developing your personality behind the bar is like an actor developing their character profile; the bar is your stage so always give a great performance. This can be demonstrated in the smallest of ways, from the flourish in presenting a bottle of beer and glass and bringing them together neatly on a napkin, to the way in which you pour, shake and make your drinks. A guest can be entertained in so many ways; a simple flip of a shaker or a long pour will impress most customers.

To deliver impeccable service you must ensure that the guest leaves feeling delighted that you took the standard of service that one step further. This can be through interaction, bar tricks, light humour, general conversation and occasional flairing. Flairing is becoming increasingly popular with successful bars; the simplest of moves can have the largest impact on a guest's experience – practise the moves and only when you have mastered them and feel confident, try them out and see the response you get.

Thank you

A simple thank you to the customer after serving them is common for bartenders to forget. When returning change to a customer or completing an order always remember to thank them.

Customer care

Once you have served the drinks, check back to the customer and ask them if everything is OK. Interacting with your customer is not a crime, neither is being friendly! Care, really care, and care some more about each and every person that enters your establishment. A customer's experience in your bar is largely your responsibility. Be aware of the needs of all your customers, not just those that tip, as all customers are potential tippers and regulars. Anticipate your customers' requirements and be attentive to their needs.

Remembering a customer's drink is not only courteous but also shows professionalism. Make a mental note, or if you didn't serve the customer first time around, use your product knowledge to identify a drink by the glass in which it is served, the garnish or the colour. But if in any doubt, don't be afraid to double-check the order with your guest.

> **BARTENDER'S TIP:** If a glass looks like it's nearing empty, offer the customer another drink. It is important to remember what the drink was, and ask 'Would you like another drink?' or, for a more subtle approach, 'Same again?'. A general rule is to offer when the glass is no more than a quarter full, but remember not to be pushy – use your charm and charisma instead!

The farewell

Say goodbye to all customers, not just those you have served. Say such farewells as 'See you again', 'Thanks, have a great night', 'Cheers, see you soon' or 'Enjoy the rest of the day/evening/night'. A friendly farewell will leave a positive impression on your customers.

Repeat visits

If the drinks are served correctly and to the highest possible standard of service and a bit extra, you can guarantee you will have customers flocking back to your bar. The customer journey does not end when they leave your bar for the very first time, it continues with them in the conversations they have with work colleagues, friends, family and anyone else they share their experience with of your service and the bar that they met you in.

Considerations of the customer journey

The service that you provide should be a personal service that is tailored to each guest and adapted to the venue, without compromising consistency. It is common sense that a more formal bar, such as one found in a five-star hotel, may require a more formal approach to a loud, very large nightclub.

It is vital to also take into consideration the type of customers you are serving, as every customer will have different expectations and needs. Reading your clientele is an important skill of a professional bartender and the ability to adapt your style of service to meet and exceed all of your customers' needs is not an easy task.

HANDLING COMPLAINTS

Nobody likes receiving complaints, but complaints are not always a bad thing as they can help you improve the standard of service. No single business in any industry can say that they have never received any complaints. If we learn to handle them correctly and professionally we can increase our customer base and revenues and turn a customer's negative experience into a positive one.

A customer who complains encourages you to do your best and to keep your standards high. Your customers can see things that you might miss or not be aware of and every complaint will give you insight into how you can help to improve your business. Getting defensive never helps and almost always makes matters worse. This is not about who is right and who is wrong; it is about helping a disappointed customer and keeping their business. Remember to keep things on a professional level at all times.

Only 5% of disgruntled customers ever make their dissatisfaction known to the average business and a large portion of them will not visit or buy from that business again. Almost three quarters of customers that complain will continue to do business in your establishment if that complaint is resolved and almost all will if that complaint is handled swiftly and professionally. So follow the 10 commandments of complaint handling (see right) and remember that complaints are also feedback on the performance of your business.

Statistics show that about seven out of 10 complaining customers will do business with you again if you resolve the complaint in their favour. A study by the US News and World Report helps us to understand some of the reasons why customers decide not to return to an establishment:

- 68% due to an attitude of indifference towards the customer by employees
- 14% due to product dissatisfaction
- 9% for competitive reasons
- 5% develop other friendships and as a consequence frequent other establishments
- 1% die

10 COMMANDMENTS FOR COMPLAINT HANDLING

1. Always be polite
2. Listen attentively and do not interrupt
3. Never make excuses, blame someone or something else, argue with the guest, or raise your voice
4. Apologise but do not try to justify the situation
5. Reiterate the problem to the guest to ensure full understanding
6. Offer options to solve the problem. Agree a course of action with the guest
7. Deal with the situation immediately and efficiently
8. Thank them for bringing the situation to your attention
9. Always ensure that your guest is totally satisfied with the situation
10. Always inform a manager of important issues

Finally... never, ever take a complaint personally.

THE BAR ENVIRONMENT

THE BAR ENVIRONMENT

When setting up and preparing any work environment, a tidy, well organised space is important for productivity and speed, even more so in a service environment where you are in the spotlight. This chapter presents a basic template of a full working station of a cocktail bar.

BARTENDER'S TIPS:

• Always face the customer when preparing drinks. Customers love to see what goes into their drinks and it's also an opportunity to show off your skills!

• It is imperative that all napkins, straws and sip straws are continuously replenished throughout the course of a shift.

• Always clean shakers, mixing glasses, bar spoons, muddlers, strainers and fine strainers immediately after use. It is also vital to the smooth running of the station that the bar equipment is cleaned and placed back in its rightful place.

• If drip mats are full of liquid at the end or during the shift this means only one thing... spillage. Make sure you check all drip mats at the end of each shift; spotless drip mats are a true sign of a proficient, accurate and professional bartender.

THE STATION STRUCTURE

There are three main sections to the workstation of a contemporary bar: the service area, the station and the back bar.

The service area

The service area, also known as the bar top, is where all drinks are prepared. The service area should stock all the bar requisites and a number of necessary tools, including a bar caddy, straws, sip straws, napkins, muddler, bar spoon, strainer, Boston shakers, mixing glasses and bar mats. The above

shows how most professional bar station areas should look, some may vary depending on the environment so use this as a guide.

The station area

When setting up and preparing each cocktail station try to follow a similar structure to the one described here. This will help with the efficiency of preparing all types of drink, not just cocktails. Every bar will have its own layout with its own glassware, post-mix machines, house brands, juices, fruits, condiments and selection of tools, depending on the type of drinks menu that is on offer, so it is imperative that the station be ultra-organised at all times.

ICE AND ICE DUMP

The ice dump is the storage space within the bar workstation that holds large quantities of ice. Always ensure you have plenty of ice, both cubed and crushed, at all times. If a glass accidentally breaks in the ice, firstly alert all other team members by telling them and marking the ice with a large red X, usually with grenadine or cranberry juice. The entire ice dump will then need to be cleaned immediately, by emptying its entire contents and thoroughly cleaning out small shards of glass.

JUICE BOX

This area contains the majority of juices, purées and bottled sodas. Store-and-pours range from 1 to 5 litres (around 1.5 to 8.5 pints) and are generally used to dispense juices quickly and more efficiently.

POST-MIX MACHINE

This machine generally dispenses carbonates, including soda, cola, lemonade, and in some cases still water and tonic, depending on the outlet. This is primarily used for speed of service, not necessarily for quality, and is generally fitted to the right-hand side of the station and sometimes to both sides for optimal efficiency so that two bartenders can work a station. They are fitted with a long hose that should be able to stretch across your entire station.

SINK

Sinks are an integral part of a bartender's workstation and are used for cleaning bar equipment, washing hands, pouring slops and discarding liquids and used ice. When making cocktails, fresh fruits and herbs may need to be discarded into the sink. If this is the case, always ensure a sink strainer is in the plug to avoid blockage.

SPEEDRAILS

An essential part of any bar, speedrails are where spirit bottles are placed for efficiency and ease of access. The main purpose of a speedrail is to speed up service and it should hold the most popular/house spirits and liqueurs served. Each bar's speedrail will stock different brands, however, most will have one of the six main spirit categories: vodka, gin, rum, tequila, whisky and brandy.

BARTENDER'S TIPS:

• When using bottles and juices make sure that you replace them in their appropriate position; this is essential as they are set out for efficiency.

• If, for some reason, ice, fruit, bottle tops or any other object falls into the speedrail be sure to remove it immediately.

• Some bars will have more comprehensive bar stations than others and all bars will be entirely unique in design and operational efficiency.

• As with all operations, the speedrail will be altered according to the changes and popularity of the cocktails and spirits being served. It is common sense to place a spirit or liqueur into the speedrail if it becomes popular, rather than leaving it on the back bar.

BARTENDER'S TIPS:

• Always be sure to store glassware in order of size, with the smallest nearest to the ice dump. This will avoid knocking over taller glassware.

• Only stack glassware that can be easily separated, and be sure not to stack more than three glasses high. Stemmed glassware should never be stacked.

THE BACK BAR TOP

The back bar top generally houses the majority of the spirits and liqueurs. This area is used for point of sale and will tend to have either shelves or steps to display bottles. All areas of the back bar should be kept clean and organised, and everything should have a place and be put back in its rightful place during service.

FRIDGES

There are dozens of types of fridge used in the modern bar: glass-fronted fridges allow the customer to see what is on offer, while enclosed stainless steel ones mean that the bartender must sell or advise customers of what is on sale. Dump fridges – deep fridges that store large quantities of bottled beers – provide optimal efficiency and speed for venues with a large output.

Fridges are primarily used to chill and store pre-packaged products, such as bottles of beer, Ready-to-Drink (RTD's) and Premium Packaged Spirits (PPS's). They are also used to store bottled juices and carbonates, wines, Champagne and opened juices overnight. Martini glasses can also be stored in fridges to ensure that the customer receives a beautifully chilled drink; some bars even have freezers to store glassware.

GLASS RACK

Glass racks and shelf layout will also be unique to each bar, however, regardless of glassware design and styles there are common types that are almost always used in cocktail bars: beer glass, rocks glass, Collins glass, wine glass (red and white), and Martini glass. (See Glassware, pages 36–40, for a full breakdown of glassware styles and types.)

The back bar

The back bar is the area of the bar that stocks premium spirits, liqueurs, aperitifs, wines, champagne, point of sale (POS) products, fridges, glassware, cigars, coffee machines and sometimes snacks.

TOOLS OF THE TRADE

As a bartender, you should have a good understanding of how the bar is set up and how all the various equipment and tools look and operate. Always buy the best equipment you can afford – quality equipment will always last longer.

Bar sieve (1): used to double strain those finer cocktails, to remove shards of ice and small bits of fruit. It is used in conjunction with a Boston shaker and a Hawthorne strainer.

Bar spoon (2): a versatile stainless steel tool that has various uses. It can be used as a measuring spoon (holds approximately 5 ml), a stirrer and a layering spoon.

Boston shaker/tin and mixing glass (3): ingredients for mixing drinks are poured into the mixing glass, ice is added and the stainless steel Boston shaker caps over the top of the mixing glass to form a seal.

Bottle pourers/tapered pour-spouts (4): stainless steel pour spouts are preferred and the 285-50 model is known for its consistent quality and pour speed, and used to free-pour on regular 750-ml and 1-litre spirit, liqueur and smaller cordial bottles. The 285-60 model pour-spout has a larger diameter cork to fit an oversized bottle neck, such as some aged rums and tequilas.

Bottle opener/bar blade (5): the first tool of the bartender is the stainless steel beer bottle opener, used as an efficient tool for opening beers at speed.

Gas torch (6): torches come in various sizes and a small gas torch is the preferred choice for bartenders to brûlee foams and caramelise fruit garnishes.

Hawthorne strainer (7): for straining ice and fruit from a Boston shaker. Other uses include separating egg yolk from egg white by cracking the egg into the spring side of the strainer and draining the egg white into a container. Remove the spring of the strainer and add it to a shaker with egg white or pineapple juice. Cap with a mixing glass, shake and the spring will act as a whisk.

Jigger (8): stainless steel thimble measure used for measuring liquids. Sizes vary from 5 to 175 ml (1 tsp to 6 fl oz) in the UK and are government stamped. Jiggers should be rinsed out thoroughly after every use, and if using cream liqueurs or strong flavours, such as aniseed liqueurs, ensure they are completely clean so as not to taint the next pour.

Juicer (9): for small quantities, there are a number of handheld tools used for juicing citrus fruits. Cut the fruit in half across the equator, then juice using a citrus reamer (wooden or stainless steel). Reamers offer a way of juicing citrus fruits quickly and effectively: its pointed end ensures that every drop of juice is extracted. A citrus press is also a useful tool: place the halved fruit cut side down onto the holes and squeeze the handles together tightly to extract all the juice. An electric juicer is useful when preparing large quantities.

BARTENDER'S TIPS:
• Always keep the fridge door closed when not in use to keep the contents cold at all times.

• Stock rotation is vital to the smooth running of a bar. When restocking a fridge ensure that the new stock is put at the back of the fridge and the cold stock is brought to the front.

• Always keep fridges clean and tidy.

• Never over-fill a fridge or stack bottles side by side in an upright fridge. Never lay opened products on their side, including wines, store-and-pours and milk.

Julep strainer (10): the julep strainer is used in conjunction with a mixing glass for straining ice and fruit.

Lighter (11): every bartender should have one. A versatile tool used to make flambé garnishes, sprinkle cinnamon through and light candles.

Muddler (12): a commonly used blunt tool used to crush fruits to release juices and oils to flavour cocktails. It can also be used to crush ice in combination with a Boston shaker (see page 31). Muddlers come in many shapes and sizes, generally plastic or wooden, but you can also use a piece of sugar cane for an authentic Caipirinha or Mojito.

Pineapple corer (13): used to hollow out pineapples so that the shell can be used as a drinking vessel. Remove the head of the pineapple with a sharp knife and use the corer to twist the flesh out of the fruit, leaving the core and the skin.

Tongs (14): used for handling fruit garnishes. Larger bar tongs are used for handling ice.

Waiter's friend (15): a very useful tool of the trade as it fulfils a number of uses, including cutting foil from wine bottles, as well as opening wine and beer bottles.

Whisk (16): mainly used for whipping up egg white to use in cocktails.

Zester (17): a great bar tool used for peeling the zest of citrus fruit. The small sharp holes on the end of the tool are used for making fine shavings and the larger tooth is used to cut thin strips of citrus peel, which can then be used to make citrus spirals, knots and other fancy garnishes.

Pens: a bartender always needs three pens: one to use, one to lose and one to give away.

BAR PREPARATION

Before the bar opens for busy trade, it is important that you stock-up appropriately to ensure the smooth running of the bar throughout service. A poorly prepared bar can cause strain to service and unnecessary delays during busy periods.

Opening duties

All opening duties should be performed while the bar is closed so when the first customer arrives you are 100 per cent ready for full service. Follow this basic opening checklist and adapt it to your working environment.

Opening checklist
✔ Switch on lights, fridge lights, glass washer, blenders, coffee machine and any other electrical equipment.
✔ Place bar floor matting out.
✔ Prepare all bins and bottle bins.
✔ Count till register float and prepare change.
✔ Prepare beer drip trays and replace beer taps.
✔ Pull through a small amount of the most popular beers to check they haven't run out and are flowing nicely.
✔ Check fridge stock levels and ensure they are all fully stocked.
✔ Check back-up stock levels.
✔ Replace and organise pouring spirits in speedrail ready for service.
✔ Prepare fresh juices, purées and sodas.
✔ Prepare sugar syrup (if made fresh).
✔ Open house wines if necessary.
✔ Prepare garnishes.
✔ Organise glassware.
✔ Give the bar top a thorough clean.
✔ Set up the bar service area, ensuring bar caddies are full with napkins and straws.
✔ Put out drinks/food menus on the bar and tables.
✔ Ensure all tools are clean.
✔ Finally, fill ice wells.

CRUSHED ICE
Crush small quantities of ice by placing ice cubes in a Boston shaker and crush with a large muddler. For venues that require large quantities of crushed ice, a commercial ice crusher is recommended.

LEMON AND LIME JUICES

Whenever possible always prepare lemon and lime juices fresh for every shift. When juicing citrus fruit, ensure it is not straight from the fridge or freezer as cold fruit produces less juice.

Roll the fruit to extract more juice, then cut in half using a sharp knife.

For small quantities, juice with a handheld juicer (reamer).

For larger quantities, use an electric juicer, then fine strain into a juice pourer or an empty thoroughly clean spirit bottle to ensure there are no pips or large pieces of fruit.

HOMEMADE SUGAR SYRUP

Sugar syrup can be made using any type of sugar, including granulated, caster sugar, demerara sugar or muscovado sugar. Also known as simple syrup, sugar syrup is a staple ingredient in cocktails and is the most practical and cost-effective sweetener. White granulated sugar is most commonly used to make sugar syrup so that the resulting syrup is clear and does not affect the colour of the cocktail. It is commonly used with clear spirits, such as gin, vodka, white rum and white tequila.

Demerara sugar is the generic name of a type of specialty raw cane sugar often used in home baking and for sweetening coffee. Demerara sugar is light brown in colour (the natural colour of cane sugar) and quite coarse, and is generally used with aged spirits such as aged rums, reposado and anejo tequilas, dark rums, whiskies and cognacs.

Muscovado sugar is a type of unrefined sugar with a strong flavour of molasses. Also known as Barbados or moist sugar, it is dark brown and slightly coarser and stickier than most brown sugars.

Use a dry plastic funnel or a homemade paper funnel to half fill an empty sterile glass bottle with your choice of sugar.

Fill to about 90 per cent with warm water (boiled first, then left to cool a little). Shake vigorously for 1 to 2 minutes or until the sugar is fully dissolved, then top up with cold water and add a pour spout. If stored in the fridge, sugar syrup can keep for up to two weeks.

HOMEMADE FLAVOURED SYRUPS

Honey syrup is a popular substitute for sugar syrup and is prepared and stored in the same way. Use the best possible clear, runny honey and simply pour the honey straight into a bottle, add boiled water left to cool a little and dissolve. Honey comes in dozens of varieties and it's worth experimenting with different types. Manuka or acacia honey both work fantastically well in mixed drinks. Other ingredients that make interesting pouring syrups are treacle, maple and golden syrups.

SPICE, HERB AND FRUIT SYRUPS

There are many spices that can be used to make flavoured syrups. Some of the most popular include vanilla, cinnamon, juniper berries, cardamom and root ginger. To make vanilla syrup, add two or three spilt vanilla pods to a bottle of sugar syrup. With cinnamon, juniper and cardamom you must first crack the spices before placing them in the bottle. Herbs are simply placed in the bottle but be sure to remove the stalks as they can add a bitter flavour. For ginger syrup, add thin slivers of root ginger to sugar syrup. Shake the bottle regularly and leave the flavours to infuse for several days before using.

To make fruit syrups, heat sugar syrup in a saucepan and add your chosen fruit to the pan. Strawberries, raspberries, blackberries and blackcurrants work particularly well, as do the sweeter tropical fruits such as pineapples and honeydew melons. Mash the fruit and reduce the liquid until a thick but runny syrup is achieved. The liquid should then be fine strained into an empty sterile bottle.

COMMERCIAL SYRUPS

Commercial sugar syrup is more commonly referred to as gomme syrup, gum syrup or sirop de gomme and contains preservatives and sometimes orange blossom. In practice it is easier and flavour consistent to use commercial fruit syrups, which come in hundreds of flavours, the most popular being grenadine (made from the juice of pomegranate) and orgeat (almond extract). Commercial syrups also have a longer shelf life than homemade syrups.

BARTENDER'S TIPS:

• The shelf life of homemade syrups will depend on how long they are left out at room temperature and if they are stored in a refrigerator overnight. Syrups can last from one week to several weeks.

• Always check homemade syrups for any moss or mould on the surface as this is a sign of bacteria so discard these immediately.

• Demerara sugar takes its name from the Demerara colony in Guyana, which was the original source of this type of sugar, but it is mainly produced in Mauritius now.

Bar keep and cleanliness

It is essential to keep the station organised at all times to ensure optimum operational efficiency. Keeping the bar spotless even during busy periods is a sign of a professional bartender. A clean area is inviting to the guest – a wet, sticky bar top is a definite turn-off and will not inspire confidence in your customers.

Don't use wads of beverage napkins to wipe down the bar or to mop up spillages as they are expensive and should only be used to present drinks on; cloths are used for cleaning the bar; make sure these are rinsed and changed on a regular basis.

Always offer a fresh napkin with every drink served. Replenish straws, napkins, ice, fruit, juices, glassware and tools often – this can be done during service too.

When using a cocktail shaker it must be cleaned immediately after use, especially when using dairy products, such as milk and cream. Jiggers or spirit measures should also be washed out after each cocktail has been made, using soda flash-spray or water. Soda is great for cleaning any metallic/stainless steel equipment, such as jiggers and shakers. Bar spoons should be cleaned and placed back in their appropriate home.

Pasteurised carton juices have a shelf life of approximately two to three days, which means that you need to monitor when they are poured into the pour-and-store. Pour-and-stores should be washed out thoroughly on a regular basis.

A mantra used in most professional cocktail bars is the Clean As You Go (CAYG). This enables you to keep on top of your job and ensures that the bar is kept clean at all times.

Closing duties

Closing the bar is as important as preparing the bar, and completing this undertaking properly makes everyone's life a lot easier in the long run and will make opening procedures smoother.

Breaking down the bar should be done quickly, efficiently and thoroughly. This part of the job is as integral to the smooth operation of the bar as the opening procedures and will ensure the bar is kept clean, tidy and looking professional.

Closing checklist

✔ Thoroughly clean mixing glasses and shaker tins and allow to drain. Wash all bar mats.

✔ Remove bar caddies to the back bar and replenish completely with straws, napkins and sip straws.

✔ Remove bar menus and clean.

✔ Ensure all tools are clean.

✔ Store juices, purées, sodas and syrups in the fridge and discard those that are no longer fresh and that have passed their sell-by date.

✔ Refrigerate any opened house white wines, replacing corks or wine stoppers.

✔ Discard or store garnishes in the fridge.

✔ Remove all pour spouts from creamy and coloured spirits, clean with a soda flash-spray and replace.

✔ Remove all speedrail spirits to the back bar, marry-up spirits if necessary and clean the speedrail thoroughly.

✔ Wipe down all bottles with a damp cloth.

✔ Empty all ice wells completely using the scoop, then dry out the ice well with paper towels as stale water attracts barflies.

✔ Clean beer drip trays and beer taps.

✔ Remove all glassware to the back bar, rinse and clean shelf mats and surfaces.

✔ Clean all stainless steel surfaces thoroughly.

✔ Polish any stemmed glasses with a clean, dry glass cloth.

✔ Ensure glasses are clean and replace in appropriate place.

✔ Wipe down the back bar service area and ensure the display looks perfect.

✔ Cash-up the till register and sign off with the manager.

✔ Check fridge stock levels and ensure they are all fully stocked.

✔ Switch off fridge lights, glass washer, blenders, coffee machine and any other electrical equipment.

The following closing duties should only be done once all the above tasks have been completed:

✔ Empty all bins and bottle bins.

✔ Clean and dry all bar service areas.

✔ Set up the service area for the next session and ensure you polish the shaker tins.

✔ Remove bar matting from the bar area.

✔ Clean floors appropriately with dustpan and brush.

✔ Mopping should be the last job of the breakdown.

GLASSWARE

Glassware that is spotlessly clean shows off all drinks to great advantage.

Always check glasses for lipstick marks, smears, chips and cracks before using. This should be done subtly and professionally by simply holding the glass up to the light. If you see a smear or lipstick mark be sure to wipe the smear with a napkin and rack for cleaning. If you find a crack or a chip always throw away in a specified glass bin not the trash.

Preparing glassware

All stemmed glassware should be polished dry to avoid unsightly stains. A bar should always have an adequate supply of clean glasses to avoid using recently washed warm glasses, which can cause thermal shock. Thermal shock is when a glass shatters due to a sudden extreme change in temperature. To avoid thermal shock place a bar spoon into the glass – the steel will absorb the shock.

Before using glassware ensure that it is at room temperature. Make sure that the correct glass is used for the correct drink

Ideally, cold drinks should be served in cold glassware and vice versa; however, this is not always

possible in a busy bar. Martini glasses should always be chilled before use.

Handling glassware

Handling glassware correctly is not only important for reasons of hygiene but also avoids leaving unsightly finger marks on the glass. Never pick up or hold clean glasses by the rim. Handling glassware appropriately demonstrates a good level of etiquette and professionalism.

Stemmed glassware should only be handled by the stem.

All other glassware should be handled on the bottom half.

Multiple glass pick-up

Speed and efficiency are key in a busy bar when making multiple orders. Picking up glassware in twos and threes to prepare drinks is one way of being more efficient. This can only be done with stemless glassware, such as rocks, Collins, beer and highball glasses.

Two-glass pick-up: grasp one glass with your thumb and forefinger and the other with the butt of the hand and your little finger.

Three-glass pick-up: the same technique as above applies, but use your middle finger to secure the third glass against the other two and grip tightly, bringing all three glasses together.

GLASSWARE STYLES

Here are some examples of the most popular types of glassware used in bars today. It is worth noting that no glass should be filled to the brim and that the liquid capacity of a glass filled with regular ice differs to that of one filled with crushed ice. As a general rule of thumb, a glass filled with regular ice cubes will require approximately half the liquid volume of the glass; one filled with crushed ice, a third. Don't forget to allow for lip space in all cases!

Mixing glass

Also known as the Boston glass, this is the most commonly used glass for making cocktails, although it is never used to serve drinks in, but rather to mix drinks. It has a conical shape with a toughened heavy base and is used in conjunction with a Boston shaker.

Size range: 16 fl oz
Drinks served in this glass: only used for mixing and preparing drinks, never use as a drinking vessel.

Rocks glass

These glasses are generally used for serving a single spirit and a mixer, and cocktails served in these glasses are generally a little stronger than drinks served in tall glasses. Commonly used for drinks served on the rocks or frappéd (over crushed ice). This glass should also have a toughened base, which is ideal for drinks that require muddling and are often used instead of an old-fashioned glass.

Size range: 8–10 fl oz
With regular ice and lip space: 4–5 fl oz
With crushed ice and lip space: 3 fl oz
Drinks served in this glass: single spirit and a mixer, Caipirosca, Russians, Margarita on the rocks, Daiquiri on the rocks.

Old fashioned glass

Old fashioned glasses, such as tumblers, lowballs or short glasses, are commonly used for serving neat spirits and are sometimes used in the same way as rocks glasses and visa versa. They are a slightly different shape to a rocks glass, usually with straight sides but generally the same size. This glass takes its name from the best known cocktail served in it, the Old Fashioned.

Size range: 8–10 fl oz
With regular ice and lip space: 4–5 fl oz
With crushed ice and lip space: 3 fl oz
Drinks served in this glass: neat spirits, Sazerac, Sours, Old Fashioned.

Collins glass

These glasses, also called highball glasses, are most commonly used to make highballs (double spirits and a mixer), and tall cocktails. A 12 oz glass is also perfect for a regular 330 ml bottle of beer.

Size range: 12–14 fl oz
With regular ice and lip space: 6–7 fl oz
With crushed ice and lip space: 3–4 fl oz
Drinks served in this glass: Highballs, Breezes, Iced teas, Mexican Mule, Mojito, Juleps, Collins.

Martini glass

The Martini glass, also known as a cocktail or classic glass, is an iconic symbol of style. Drinks served in Martini glasses should always be served without ice – the ice should only be used to chill the glass – and should also never be served with a straw. When a drink calls to be served straight-up, up, classic or Martini, then this is the glass of choice.

Size range: 5 or 7 fl oz
Capacity and liquid volume: only add 3 fl oz (for a 5¼ fl oz glass) or 4½ fl oz (for a 7 fl oz glass) of liquid to a mixing glass, as a drink served in a Martini glass is either stirred or shaken with ice, which will cause dilution that can add 1–2 fl oz of liquid. This will also leave enough lip space.
Drinks served in this glass: Dry Martini, Manhattans, Daiquiri Straight-Up, Cosmopolitan, Margarita Straight-Up, Fruit Martinis.

Margarita glass

Taken from the cocktail of the same name, this margarita or coupette glass is generally used to serve frozen margaritas and daiquiris and has a broad-rim for holding salt. Regular ice is not ideally used with this glass because of the shape but it is ideal for serving most frozen drinks.

Size range: 8–10 fl oz
With regular ice and lip space: 4–5 fl oz
With crushed ice and lip space: 2–3 fl oz
Drinks served in this glass: frozen drinks and drinks served on crushed ice, frozen margaritas, frozen daiquiris.

Sling glass

This tall, thin Pilsner glass also takes its name from the famous cocktail the Singapore Sling, a fantastic glass to showcase drinks with fresh fruit, such as Pimm's, and can be used with regular and crushed ice. Quality commercial sling glasses will have a thick heavy base and a short stem.

Size range: 11 fl oz
No ice to the brim: 11 fl oz
With regular ice and lip space: 5 fl oz
With crushed ice and lip space: 3 fl oz
Drinks served in this glass: Singapore Sling, slings, Russian Spring Punch, Long Island.

Hurricane glass

These glasses, also referred to as Pina Colada, Poco Grande and Zombie glasses, are generally used to make the cocktails of the same name. The distinct pear-shaped curve of this glass is reminiscent of vintage hurricane lamps and range in size from 10 to 20 fl oz.

Size range: 10–20 fl oz
With regular ice and lip space: 5–10 fl oz
With crushed ice and lip space: 3–7 fl oz
Drinks served in this glass: Pina Colada, flavoured coladas, Zombies, Blue Hawaiian, other tropical drinks.

Brandy balloon glass

Also known as a snifter glass, this glass is primarily used to serve cognac or other brandies. The large bowl collects the aromas of the drink and the more expensive the brandy the larger the glass. These glasses are also ideal for pouring flamed drinks from.

Size range: 6–60 fl oz
Drinks served in this glass: brandy only.

Pousse-café or shot glass

These glasses come in a number of shapes and sizes but generally contain between 1 and 2½ fl oz. Used to prepare shooters/pousse cafés and single shots served straight, without ice.

Size range: 1–2 fl oz
Drinks served in this glass: spirits served neat, Flaming B52.

White wine glass

Selecting the right wine glass for a wine style is important, as the shape of the glass can influence the taste of the wine. White wine glasses are generally narrower than red wine glasses, although not as narrow as champagne flutes. The narrowness of the white wine glass allows the chilled wine to retain its temperature. Also, the smaller bowl means less contact between the hand and the glass, and so body heat does not transfer as easily to the wine. The white wine glass is sometimes used in replacement of a margarita glass to serve frozen and ice cream cocktails.

Size range: 8–24 fl oz and sometimes larger
Drinks served in this glass: white wine, frozen drinks, ice cream drinks, frozen daiquiris and margaritas.

Red wine glass

Glasses for red wine are generally characterised by their rounder, larger bowl, which allows the wine to breathe. As most reds are meant to be consumed at room temperature, the wider bowl allows the wine to cool more quickly after hand contact has warmed it. Red wine glasses can also have their own particular styles, such as Bordeaux glasses, which are tall with a wide bowl, and are designed for full-bodied wines like Cabernet and Merlot as they direct wine to the back of the mouth. Burgundy glasses are larger than Bordeaux glasses and have a larger bowl to collect aromas of more delicate red wines such as Pinot Noir. This style of glass directs wine to the tip of the tongue.

Size range: 8–16 fl oz
Drinks served in this glass: red wine only.

Champagne flute

This glass is primarily used to serve champagne or Champagne cocktails. The classic julep shape gives length to the bubbles of the drink. Champagne cocktails should never contain ice as this spoils the champagne.

Size range: 6–8 fl oz
Drinks served in this glass: Bellinis, classic Champagne, French 75, Kir Royale, Bubbling Berries.

Port glass
A traditional port glass holds 6.5 fl oz (185 ml) and is 15 cm (6 in) high. It is shaped like a small version of a red wine glass.

Size range: 6½ fl oz
Drinks served in this glass: port only.

Sherry glass
The Spanish-style sherry glass shown, also known as a copita, is around 15 cm (6 in) high and holds 6 fl oz (170 ml).

Size range: 6 fl oz
Drinks served in this glass: sherry only.

Pint and half-pint glasses
A standard pint glass holds an imperial pint (568 ml) of liquid and is usually used for beer or cider. Half-pint glasses hold an imperial half-pint (284 ml).

Size range: 10–20 fl oz
Drinks served in this glass: beer and cider.

Conical pint glasses
These glasses are shaped, as the name suggests, as an inverted truncated cone. They are around 15 cm (6 in) tall, tapering by about 2.5 cm (1 in) in diameter over its height. More often than not, the glass bulges out a couple of inches from the top. This is partly for improved grip and partly to prevent the glasses from sticking together when stacked.

Size range: 20 fl oz
Drinks served in this glass: beer and cider.

Toddy glass (also known as Irish coffee or latte glass). These glasses have a handle on the side and are made from toughened glass to hold hot drinks comfortably.

Size range: 8–10 fl oz
Drinks served in this glass: any hot drinks, including Irish coffee and lattes.

GARNISH PREPARATION

You should have a good range of fresh garnishes to hand. Take a trip to your local grocer and try out more exotic imported produce as well as more staple local products. When preparing garnishes always use a sharp stainless steel serrated knife and a wooden or plastic cutting board over a flat non-slip surface. To stop the board from slipping place a damp bar towel or napkin underneath it.

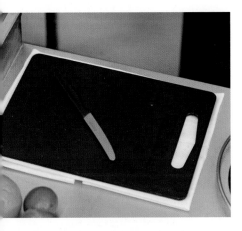

A few points to remember when preparing and presenting garnishes:

✔ A drink should always be dressed, never naked (unless it's a naked Martini).

✔ Be fussy about the quality of the fruit you select. Make sure there are no blemishes or marks and remove any stamps or stickers before cutting the washed fruit.

✔ Gain inspiration for garnishes from chefs and quality restaurants.

✔ Use the aroma of fruit, botanicals, spices and other ingredients to add to the sensory experience.

✔ Combine garnishes that are visually stimulating with edible and aromatic garnishes. E.g. juniper berries (visual), apple fan (edible) and mint sprig (aromatic).

✘ Do not overcrowd a drink with unnecessary large garnishes. Instead take a more subtle approach as less is sometimes more! This is important when using delicate Martini and Champagne glasses where aesthetically smaller garnishes work much better.

As a general rule of thumb, it is appropriate to garnish a cocktail with the flavours used in the drink. For instance, if you are making a strawberry daiquiri garnish the drink with a strawberry or alternatively a lime wedge (as a daiquiri contains lime). This helps identify the cocktail and will complement the flavours already in the drink.

Ripeness and whether the fruit is in season will change the strength of sweetness, sourness and bitterness, so always taste your fresh ingredients before using them in drinks.

The same garnishes should be uniform in size, shape and colour; consistency and continuity are important, and it stops your guests from arguing with each other over who's got the largest pineapple wedge or caramelised apple slice!

Citrus fruits

The citrus family includes limes, lemons, oranges, tangerines, satsumas, grapefruit and pink grapefruit. Citrus fruits are very versatile and can be used as garnishes in almost any bar drink.

WEDGES

Cut the ends off the fruit and cut lengthways, then cut into equal sections. Oranges and grapefruit produce rather large wedges and you can usually get between eight and 12 wedges. Use these large wedges on larger glasses, such as hurricane glasses. Limes produce approximately six wedges and lemons eight.

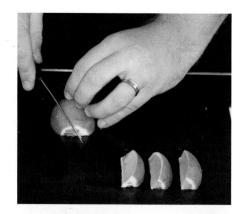

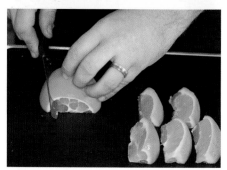

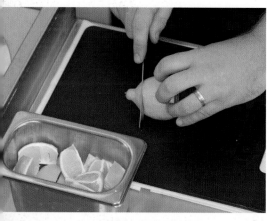

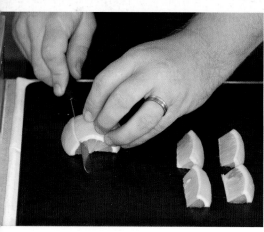

For bottled beers that require a lime wedge inserted in the neck of the bottle, cut limes into eight wedges to ensure they fit comfortably into the mouth of the bottle.

WHEELS

A wheel is a slice of fruit with a slit in it used as a garnish on the rim of a glass. You can make wheels with all citrus fruit and also with pears, apples and cucumber.

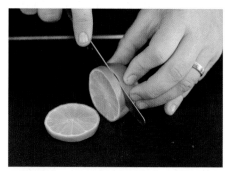

Cut the ends off the fruit and slice widthways so that each slice is about 0.5 cm (³⁄₈ in) thick.

To make a slice, make a wheel and then cut the wheel in half.

For quarters, make a slice and then cut the segment in half again.

SPIRALS

A spiral is a citrus garnish in the shape of a spring that is both pleasing to the eye and gives a drink a beautiful aroma.

Use a canelle knife to cut a long length of thin peel. Start at the top of the fruit and make a small insertion with the tooth of the knife, then drag the tooth under the skin of the fruit. Use your thumb and forefinger to hold the fruit firmly and then twist your other hand, not the fruit. Use a straw to twist the spiral around to make a tight springy spiral. Thick and tight-skinned citrus fruit, such as lemons or oranges work best for this garnish. Over-ripened fruits tend not to work as well. Spirals can also be used to make knots and other garnish presentations.

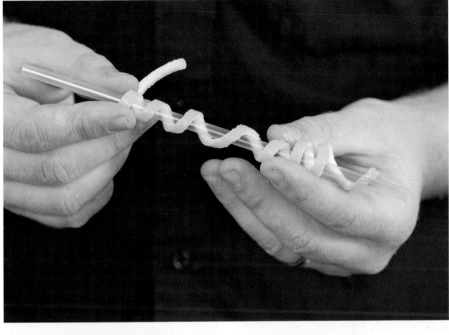

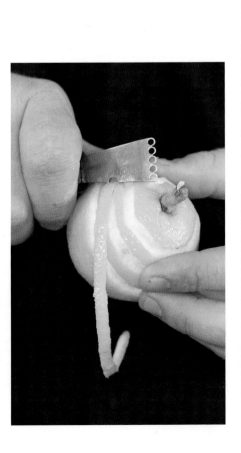

TWISTS

A twist is a 1–2 mm thick strip of citrus skin used to spray oils onto the surface of a drink. It is used in drinks such as the Vodka Martini (lemon twist) and the Cosmopolitan (orange twist).

Cut a skin-deep strip approximately 3–4 cm (1¼ in) long from any citrus fruit. Be sure not to cut too deep into the fruit as the pith can be bitter and affect the taste of the drink. The oils in the skin of citrus fruit give an amazing aroma and flavour to drinks.

A theatrical way of spraying aromatic oils of fruit onto the surface of drinks. The oils in citrus fruit can impact a drink's flavour and aroma immensely. Spraying the oils through a flame and onto a drink adds a little theatre and can give a slight burned taste and aroma.

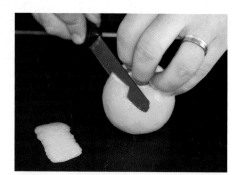

OTHER GARNISHES

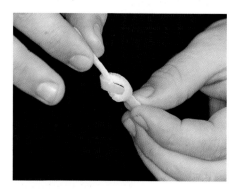

Knot: a small spiral of citrus rind tied into a knot.

Horse's neck: similar to a spiral but with a 3–4 cm (1½ in) piece of the fruit kept on.

Wedge with mint sprig: cut a hole in the skin of a citrus wedge and insert the stem of a mint sprig and then fan. Ideal for crushed ice drinks.

Citrus shavings: small shavings of citrus fruit, presented on drinks with crushed ice or on drinks served in Martini glasses.

Tree fruits

Tree fruits include apples, pears, plums, cherries, peaches, nectarines and apricots. Tree fruits can be used in all manner of garnishes. Here is a selection of contemporary cocktail garnishes.

FRUIT FAN

Cut the fruit into 0.5 cm (¼ in) thick slices and use two, three or four slices to fan the fruit. Apples, pears and strawberries work well in combination with other garnishes, such as mint sprigs.

CARAMELISED SLICES

Pears and apples, along with citrussy oranges, lemons, limes and grapefruit all work really well caramelised with demerara sugar, but be sure not to burn the sugar! To caramelise fruit, simply sprinkle sugar liberally over the fruit or dip into a bowl of sugar, then using a chef's torch, heat the sugar using the tip of the flame until the sugar bubbles and starts to colour. Repeat on the other side. When cooled the sugar will harden to the fruit.

Soft fruits

Soft fruits, or berry fruits, include strawberries, raspberries, blackberries, blackcurrants, redcurrants, gooseberries, loganberries, cloudberries, cranberries, grapes and any other edible berries.

Berry and mint sprig: best made with raspberries and blackberries with a mint sprig inserted in the centre of the berry.

Tropical and unusual fruits

These fruits always add a touch of glamour to a drink. They include melon, passion fruit, kiwi, banana, pineapple, physalis, mango, lychee, pomegranate, star fruit and many more.

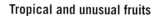

Berry sail: take a citrus wheel and make a cut from the centre outwards. With a cocktail stick, pierce through the flesh of the fruit close to the cut and rind, thread on a berry, fold the wheel over, thread on another berry, fold the wheel over again and finish by piercing the flesh near the cut at the other end.

Berry kebabs: all berries can be used on a cocktail stick. Thread no more than three berries of your choice on to the stick as more would overcrowd the drink.

Redcurrant and cranberry bunch: hang a small bunch of redcurrants or cranberries over the side of a glass to make a pretty, colourful garnish.

Berries dipped in chocolate: make a cut in each berry so that you can place it on the side of a glass, then freeze for a couple of hours. Melt some dark chocolate in a pan and dip the berries in the chocolate.

Grapes: use whole red or white grapes, or a mixture of both, threaded on a cocktail stick, or a single grape wedged on the side of a glass.

Melon (water, cantaloupe and honeydew): always looks great with the skin on, cut into thin strips, or quartered, sliced or wedged on the side of the glass.

Passion fruit: is often halved and the shell used as a little bowl. You can also scoop out the lush seeds for use in making drinks. The skin is not edible, but the bowl can be filled with flammable spirit and placed on top of a drink, as with the Zombie.

Banana: slice bananas at a 45-degree angle with the skin on, make a small cut from the centre and place on the side of a glass.

Physalis: keep the leaves on and open up like a flower, make a small insertion in the fruit and place on the side of a stemmed glass.

Pineapple: first cut the unpeeled pineapple into 1 cm (⅜ in) thick wheels, then cut each wheel into eighths. Make a small cut from the centre of the fruit and place on the side of a glass. The leaves can also be used for decoration.

Kiwi: leave the kiwi unpeeled and use as a wheel or slice. Prepare in the same way as citrus fruit.

Mango: mangoes can be cut into slices and wedges and it is best to keep the skin on. Make sure the fruit is thoroughly rinsed before cutting.

Lychee: make a small cut to pierce the shell of the lychee, then peel and use on the side of a glass or simply placed in a Lychee Martini.

Pomegranate: scoop out the seeds and use whole in drinks. The skin is not edible and if the seeds are crushed they give a bitter taste.

Star fruit: this unusual shaped fruit makes a pretty decoration placed on the side of a glass. Cut in the same way as a wheel to make thin stars.

Botanicals, spices and nuts

Herbs and spices add an amazing flavour and aroma to drinks. Make sure you use only fresh herbs as these will add colour and zing. Always inform customers if a drink or garnish includes nuts, in case of nut allergies.

Herbs: mint (including the various hybrid types, such as apple and pineapple), basil, coriander (seeds and leaves), thyme, lemon thyme, rosemary, lemongrass root, liquorice root, root ginger, juniper berries and many more.

Mint: there is a multitude of hybrid mints, including pineapple, apple and peppermint. Use either as an ingredient in cocktails or as an aromatic garnish. Always use fresh sprigs and the most tender leaves, or a single leaf to float on top of a drink.

Basil: as with mint, always use fresh sprigs or a single leaf to float on top of a drink.

Edible flowers: some rose, orchid, nasturtium, marigold and violet petals can be used as garnishes to float on top of drinks. Make sure you check with your supplier which flowers are edible.

Spices: vanilla pods, saffron, cinnamon sticks, nutmeg, kaffir lime leaves, black coriander, star anise, chillies (whole, flakes, powder), cardamom and cloves are just some of the spices that can be added to drinks to give aroma and flavour.

Nuts: almonds, macadamia, hazelnut, brazil, walnut, pistachio, cashew – many nuts can be used and grating is recommended.

Flavoured sugars: use demerara or muscovado sugar. Flavoured sugars can be made by adding all manner of spices and dried fruit, vanilla, cinnamon, nutmeg, almond, coconut, dried citrus peel, coffee beans and more.

UNUSUAL GARNISHES

Clove mohican: insert a row of cloves in the skin or a lime wedge, then make a small cut into the lime and place on the side of the glass or on top of the drink.

Dusting/grating: use fine powder, pepper, cocoa, chocolate or grated cinnamon, nutmeg or nuts sprinkled on the surface of a drink. You could also sprinkle through a cinnamon flame to give a slightly toasted taste and add a little theatre.

Homemade syrups: many spices can be used to make homemade syrups. Simply add the ingredient to regular sugar syrup and leave the flavours to infuse for 24 hours. You can speed up the process by capping the bottle and putting it through the dishwasher or by leaving it in a warm place.

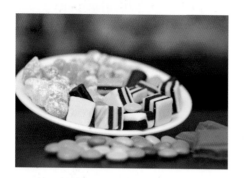

Sweets: all manner of confectionery can be used in and to garnish cocktails. Chocolate pieces, jelly sweets, fudge, bonbons, liquorice, Smarties – be imaginative and experiment, it can be quite good fun!

Biscuits: sometimes used whole with cream drinks or crumbled on top of drinks, try using Oreo cookies and Bourbon biscuits with drinks with whipped cream.

Vegetables

Olives: used to complement drinks such as martinis and those served in cocktail glasses. Preferably use threaded on a cocktail stick. The use of stuffed olives is not generally recommended for the classic Dry Martini. For a Gibson, use a couple of silver-skin onions threaded onto a cocktail stick.

Cucumber slices: slice the cucumber at a 45-degree angle with the skin on, make a small cut from the centre and place on the side of a glass. Great as a garnish for a Hendricks and Tonic or a Cucumber Martini.

Cherry tomatoes: halve and ensure the cut side is presented to the customer. Looks great as an alternative garnish for a Bloody Mary.

Celery sticks: leave the leaves on and use the stem as a stirrer in a Bloody Mary.

Preserves and condiments

There are literally hundreds of other ingredients commonly used in kitchens that can be used by the modern bartender. Don't be afraid to experiment!

Sticky stuff: honey, lemon- and lime-infused honey, chocolate spread, treacle, maple syrup, caramel, jam, marmalade and other preserves. Use to coat the inside of a glass, add to the rim and also as a covering on fruits.

Salt and pepper: sprinkle salt or pepper on the surface of a drink or use to rim the glass. Try lemon pepper, and sea/rock salt. You can also make flavoured salt with citrus fruit by drying out the skin of the fruit and muddling it with sea salt in a pestle and mortar. Orange salt works really well with Cointreau in a Margarita, and lemon salt works fantastically well with a Vanilla Margarita.

Sugar: sugar can be used to decorate drinks by sprinkling a little on top of a drink or by frosting the rim of a glass. There are many types and flavours of sugar, including, caster, demerara, muscovado, and flavoured sugar (cinnamon, vanilla and citrus to name a few).

Balsamic vinegar: a dash of balsamic reduction to a savoury drink adds an intense sweetness. To make balsamic reduction simply add balsamic vinegar to a heated saucepan and add demerara sugar and reduce to the desired sweetness/thickness.

FROSTING A GLASS

Frosting, also known as rimming, is widely used in cocktail-making. Rub the rim of a glass with a lime wedge and then dip the edge into a tray of salt, holding the glass at a 45-degree angle and ensuring the salt is added to the outside lip of the glass only. Make sure you don't salt the inside of the glass too, as you will end up with a very salty drink! Salt frosting is most popularly used for margaritas, but other ingredients, such as granulated sugar, cinnamon powder, cocoa, grated coconut and pepper are also used for frosting other drinks.

PRODUCT KNOWLEDGE

PRODUCT KNOWLEDGE

It is vital for bartenders to be familiar with the products they are selling. Being knowledgeable and having a good understanding of what you are serving will not only empower you but inspire your clientele. The following pages cover the fundamentals of product knowledge and the processes involved in its production.

SPIRITS

There are literally thousands of different types of spirit on the market, some more well known than others, and each with its very own unique taste and aroma. The raw materials used, the process of fermentation, distillation and filtration, and the amount of time a spirit is left to mature, all contribute to the very personal character of a finished product.

A brief history of spirits

A spirit is a beverage that has been produced by the process of distillation. Ever since the discovery of distillation people have been trying to produce spirits and liqueurs from all manner of ingredients, ranging from human brains, swans and crushed pearls. With this strangeness put aside, the earliest discovery of distillation was believed to be by Jabir Ibn Hayyan, a 9th century Islamic chemist who invented the alembic still. This knowledge was then brought to Europe by the Moors, circa 1300s, who widely practised in alchemy and apothecary. In the 15th and 16th centuries Italian and French monks became interested in the medicinal effects of their potions rather than the effects of alcohol, experimenting with roots, berries, grasses, herbs and peels, which gave us such liqueurs as Benedictine and Chartreuse.

Making alcohol

Ethanol, also known as ethyl alcohol or alcohol, is a flammable, tasteless, colourless, mildly toxic chemical compound with a distinctive odour, and is the alcohol found in alcoholic beverages. Ethanol, hereafter referred to as alcohol, is the natural result of a process called fermentation, which occurs when you combine starch, yeast and water. For many thousands of years, fermented drinks based on cereal (beer) or fruit (wine) were enjoyed.

Spirit production

Whichever spirit is being distilled, the basic process is the same, however, each spirit has its own distinctive character that separates it from the next, and this distinction is characterised by the following areas of the production process: raw materials, yeasts and fermentation, distillation, filtration and maturation.

RAW MATERIALS

The most important raw material used in the production of spirits and liqueurs is water. Water is used throughout the spirit production process, including fermentation and distillation, and is finally added to reduce the spirit to bottling strength. In a standard bottle of spirit with a 40% ABV (alcohol by volume) or 80% proof, the other 60% is water.

The other raw materials are starch or fermentable sugars. These are recognised as grains (barley, wheat, corn, rye and other cereals) used to make vodka, gin and whiskies; plants (agave, sugar cane, sugar beet and potatoes) used to make tequila, rum and potato vodkas; and fruits (grapes, apples, pears, cherries, apricots, plums, berry fruits and other soft tree fruits) used to make brandies/eaux de vie.

FERMENTATION

Ethanol is produced by fermentation. In order to produce ethanol, starch must first be converted into sugars. Once the raw materials have been converted into sugars, water and yeast are then added and the liquid is left to ferment from 40 hours up to a week or more. Adding yeast begins the fermentation process and is the magic ingredient in the production of alcohol. As the yeast feeds on the sugars and converts them into alcohol, gas is produced in the form of carbon dioxide. The fermentation process enhances the natural flavour of the starch, the resulting liquid is known as the 'wash or beer', and will generally have an alcoholic strength of between 7 and 11%.

DISTILLATION

The wash is then distilled in either a copper pot or column stills, or in some cases both, yielding a spirit with an ABV of between 45 and 96%. The boiling point of alcohol is 78.3°C and the alcohol rises in a vapour form. This vapour is then cooled and collected by a condenser (cooler) and as it cools it returns to a liquid form – this is the first distillation.

FILTRATION

Filtration has been used since the earliest production of alcohol and is used to remove unwanted particles or sediment and is a way to improve the quality of a spirit. There are various filters used, such as quartz sand, flint, diamond dust, cloth and more commonly activated charcoal. Depending on the spirit and distillery, filtration can be used at various stages: as the water is added, before the spirit is aged and before bottling. In modern spirit production filtration is primarily used to ensure that impurities are removed from the spirit and to enhance clarity and crispness.

MATURATION

Ageing or maturation is used for dark spirits such as rums, tequilas, whiskies and brandies. Vodka and gin are un-aged spirits. When the spirit leaves the still it is generally clear and the spirit is placed in oak barrels/casks, and ageing then takes place. The maturation process affects the spirit's final colour, aroma and taste. In many cases the majority of an aged spirit's flavour and colour is taken from the oak barrels and is generally associated to the length of time a spirit has been in a barrel. Some products, such as tequilas, are aged for up to sixty days whereas some whiskies and cognacs can be aged for decades.

Other factors that affect maturation are the type of oak, temperature, humidity, time and location of the ageing house. The casks expand and contract as a result of temperature and climate change over time, drawing the spirit into the wood in the cask and forcing it back out releasing tannins, vanillins and colour. Climate can also vary dramatically from the seasonal Highlands of Scotland (whiskies) to the humidity of the Caribbean (rum) and Mexico (tequila).

The size of the barrel and how many times it has been used can also impact on the final product. Spirits aged in a small barrel have more contact with the surface of the wood and therefore gain wood characters more quickly than spirits aged in a larger barrel. Also, some barrels may only be used once, particularly in bourbon production, and these are then sold on and used by other spirit producers; rum producers traditionally use ex-bourbon barrels and will therefore gain a little character from the bourbon.

DISTILLATION METHODS
Pot still
Pot still distillation is a traditional method that produces heavier, more flavoursome, spirits. Alembic or pot stills work in a similar way to a traditional kettle. The alcoholic liquid is put in the pot which is then sealed. Heat is applied to the base and as the mixture inside heats up, the alcohol turns into vapour. The vapour continues to get hotter until it is light enough to reach the very top of the still, which is cooler due to a jacket of cold water that cools the vapour to return it to liquid form. The liquid then enters a spirit safe where it is collected. The shape of the still can heavily influence the characters of the alcohol it produces.

The column still
The column still, also known as the continuous still, is more efficient in mass producing a lighter spirit and is far easier to control. Every time a pot still is used, the residue must be emptied and the still cleaned before moving on to the next batch. With the column still, the alcoholic liquid is pumped in via the top and steam is pumped in through the bottom. When they meet, the alcohol starts to boil and rises back up the column. As the alcohol becomes lighter and purer, the column can be set to capture the alcohol at any specific point, from 13% up to 96.4%.

When explaining ageing it is also important to recognise the Solera system which uses a series of barrels to make sherry, madeira, marsala, Spanish brandies and some rums. This ageing system typically uses a portion of the liquid from the last barrel of the series which is filled from the next-to-last barrel, and so on, until the first barrel is filled with new liquid. This allows the producers to gain similar effects of ageing in a shorter period of time.

Blending

Blending, also known as vatting, is a fine art. It is the job of the master blender to ensure that the final product is consistent, taking into consideration the complexity of woods and finishes of a particular range of casks. A blend can be taken from as little as a dozen casks up to fifty or more of varying ages. They are then left to marry in large vats from as little as two to three days up to a year or more. Blending is by no means dilution and the aim of the master blender is to produce a blend that brings out the best qualities of each of its constituent parts. The blends are then usually returned to the cask and left to marry for a period of months, before bottling.

Before the spirit is bottled, the spirit needs to be reduced to the usual bottling strength (about 40% ABV, unless the spirit is labelled cask strength), by diluting it with water. As mentioned previously water is a vital component and is integral to the taste of the final product. The spirit is then sent to the bottling line where it is pumped into glass bottles. Glass is non-reactive, other receptacles, such

as plastic, would cause a chemical change in the beverage. The bottling procedure is highly mechanised as the bottles are cleaned, filled, capped, sealed, labelled and loaded into boxes ready for distribution. This can be done at rates as high as 400 or more bottles per minute.

THE TASTING WHEEL

Product knowledge and the understanding of taste and aroma are a vital part of the professional bartender's training. As a 'chef of alcohol' you must ensure that you know your Advocaat from your Zubrowka. Spirits and liqueurs can be tasted in the same way wine is by using the nose, colour, taste and other principles used to understand flavour and aroma.

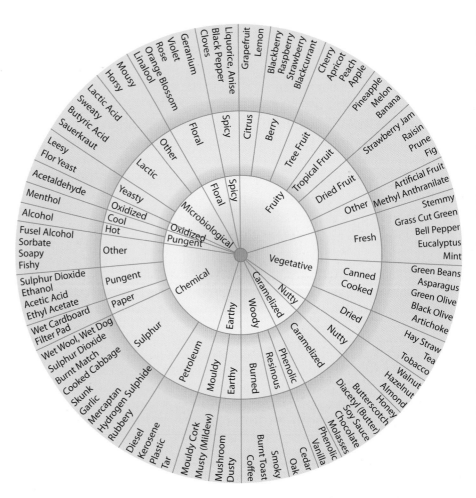

In an attempt to relate the flavours and aromas of modern spirits and liqueur ranges, this tasting wheel indicates the flavour profiles of different products.

How to taste

When tasting any spirit or liqueur it is best to use a brandy/wine glass or an ISO tasting glass to properly appreciate the aroma and colour. Add the liquid to the glass and swirl, you can then observe the 'legs' on the inside of the glass. These are indicators of sugar content; long, thick legs denote a high sugar content whereas thinner, narrower legs a lower sugar content.

Tasting begins with the nose. Take a gentle sniff of the liquid and note the initial aromas, then try again. Then draw the liquid into the mouth while breathing in at the same time and make sure the surface of the tongue is entirely coated with the liquid. At this stage it is best to make note of the initial taste and try to identify whether the liquid has a smooth, subtle, harsh or burnt taste. Note whether you taste a level of sweetness and use the tasting wheel to see if you can identify subtle flavours or aromas by using the inner circle first and working your way out. Finally, note the aftertaste as the liquid's flavours and aromas bombard your taste buds, and see how long the taste lasts on the palate.

BARTENDER'S TIPS

- Taste and aroma are completely personal and your previous experience can help to identify flavours. To develop your palate you simply need to taste and smell more, and try to register these sensations.

- When tasting products of the same category, for instance gin or vodka, try to sample at least three different brands to ensure you get a better idea of the variations in taste.

- When tasting Scotch, gin, brandy or cask-strength bourbon, you may add a little water, which can help to open up some of the finer flavours.

- Vodka, tequila, rum and standard-strength bourbons lose their aroma if diluted.

- Eating or smoking before tasting will affect your palate, so cleanse it with soda or mineral water before and in between tastings.

- Smell the back of your hand to neutralise your nasal receptors.

- Ensure you roll (not swash) the spirit around your mouth.

GRAIN DISTILLATES:

Grain distillates generally use barley, wheat, rye, corn, millet and combinations of these cereal grains in their production. Some products, such as single malt whisky, contain simply one grain, malted barley, whereas other grain distillates use a combination of grains. The 'recipe' of grains

VODKA

used is known as the mash bill. This combination or selection of grain is where the individuality of each spirit begins.

This section explores the origins, production and variety of brands that vodka has to offer. Vodka is the most consumed spirit in the world and for a spirit that has only been commercially available for the last sixty years the variety that the modern bartender has to choose from is as huge as it is interesting.

ORIGINS

The origin of vodka is an ongoing debate between the north eastern European countries of Scandinavia, Poland, Russia and Ukraine, who all lay claim to inventing modern vodka. Although vodka can be credited to one of these countries it was the Italians who brought the art of distillation to the area. It is widely known that this white neutral-tasting

spirit was first used for medicinal purposes, as well as a cologne and aftershave.

Although vodka has been produced for centuries it was only when Vladimir Smirnov fled Russia after the Bolshevik revolution that vodka started its global domination. The Smirnov family distillery was subsequently confiscated and Vladimir re-established the factory in Istanbul in 1920, but then moved back to Lviv in the Ukraine for four years and started to sell the vodka under the modern French spelling of the name Smirnoff. Another distillery

Vladimir Smirnov

was established in Paris in 1925 and by the end of 1930 it was exported throughout most of Europe.

The introduction of vodka into the American market was the result of Rudolph Kunett who purchased the rights to produce Smirnoff vodka in North America. Vodka's modern popularity can be credited to an American-invented cocktail, the Moscow Mule, which came about when an excess order of ginger beer had to be used up. It was mixed with vodka and a squeeze of lime and voilà, the Moscow Mule was born! This, along with many other notable cocktails, including the Bloody Mary and Screwdriver, helped to propel vodka into the mainstream and is now one of the most popular spirits in the world.

PRODUCTION

Vodka is generally a clear spirit that can be produced from any product that contains starch or fermentable sugar. Traditionally vodka was made using potatoes but modern vodkas are made mainly with grain, such as wheat, rye, barley, corn or a combination of grains. This combination is referred to as the 'mash bill', which is the recipe of different grains from which the spirit is made.

Once a producer has selected the raw ingredients the mash is poured into large stainless-steel vats. Yeast and water is added and the vats are closed and left to ferment for up to four days, depending on the producer and brand. Enzymes in the yeast then convert the sugars in the mash to ethyl alcohol to produce a type of beer known as the 'wash', which is between 6 and 10% ABV.

The wash is then pumped through pipes to a continuous or pot still where the magic happens. In general the majority of vodkas use continuous stills, although there are some great pot still vodkas, such as Ketel One. Once the liquid ethyl alcohol mash is pumped into stills, the alcohol is continuously cycled up and down, and heated with steam, until the vapours are released and condensed. This process also removes impurities known as congeners and ensures that the final distillate is pure and neutral. The vapours rise into the upper chambers where they are concentrated and the final distillate leaves the still up to 96.4% ABV.

The next stage is filtration which was originally used as a way of removing congeners and fusel oils (the bad stuff) that the stills couldn't. This process involves the spirit being passed through active charcoal or some other substance. Some cheaper vodkas simply steep the vodka in tanks containing charcoal.

The spirit is then watered down with demineralised water to the desired bottling strength of approximately 40% ABV/80 proof.

This pure spirit drink does not legally require anything adding to it although some producers include additives to improve the characteristics, whilst others introduce flavourings by either adding natural essences or by steeping fruits or herbs in the vodka for several days.

FLAVOURINGS

In the latter part of the 20th century, flavoured vodkas became popular, however, the practice of flavouring has been around for centuries. Herbs, grasses, spices and fruit essences may be added to the vodka after distillation. This is the fundamental difference between flavoured vodkas and other spirits with flavourings such as gin – the flavouring takes place after distillation and not during.

STYLES

There are literally thousands of vodkas available, from Absolut to Zubrowka, all with their very own unique style. Vodka styles are generally categorised by grain or potato, with there only being a handful of the latter. Given the neutrality of the spirit, the most distinctive element of vodka is the mouth feel – the texture and taste on the palate. Potato vodkas tend to be more buttery, silky and smooth, with a nutty, earthy texture. Rye vodkas tend to leave a zesty, citrus and peppery finish on the palate. Similarly, other grain vodkas can produce a myriad of aromas and textures, including floral, citrus, chemical, oily, earthy, creamy and nutty. Heat also plays a vital part in the style and quality of vodka: a smooth, rounded heat is considered a good quality finish, however, burnt, rough and raw tasting vodkas are generally cheaper.

When it comes to preference it should be left to the customer to decide; however, a little guidance should always be offered by the professional bartender.

PRICING

Pricing of spirits, as with any other product, is affected by many variables, including cost of production and materials, marketing, packaging and so on. More recently spirit brands have introduced premium and super/ultra (and ridiculously expensive) vodkas. As with age the price doesn't always guarantee a great product, and in some cases a brand will spend more effort on designing the bottle and marketing than they will on the liquid. In general though you will get what you pay for and be sure to use the best ingredients available at the right margin for your bar.

HOUSE BRANDS
Absolut (Sweden)
Altai (Serbia)
Boru (Ireland)
Danzka (Denmark)
Finlandia (Finland)
Luksusowa (Poland)
Polstar (Poland)
Smirnoff (Russia)
Stolichnaya (Russia)
Skyy (USA)
Vladivar (UK)
Wyborowa (Poland)

PREMIUM BRANDS
42 Below (New Zealand)
Belvedere (Poland)
Chopin (Poland)
Ciroc (France)
Grey Goose (France)
Ketel One (Holland)
Rain (USA)
Smirnoff Black (Russia)
Sobieski (Poland)
Wyborowa Single Estate
  (Poland)

SUPER/ULTRA PREMIUM
Diva (Scotland)
Kauffman (Russia)
Potocki (Poland)
Russky Standart (Russia)
Stolichnaya Elit (Russia)
Ultimat (Poland)
U'luvka (Poland)

ESSENTIAL SERVES

Vodka is a spirit that has traditionally been drunk on its own and ice cold, straight from a freezer. Today the majority of house vodkas are known as mixable spirits that go with most mixers; popular combinations include vodka and tonic, vodka and coke, vodka with lime and lemonade, vodka and cranberry (Cape Cod), vodka with lime and soda (Vodka Rickey) and vodka and orange (Screwdriver). The vodka contributes little in terms of flavour but gives an alcohol base.

Premium vodkas shouldn't be wasted in mixed drinks that are heavy on sugar, unless the customer requests it. Premium vodkas are generally used in classic cocktails like the Vodka Martini, or with subtle flavours or just neat.

BRANDS

When serving or mixing spirits you should always consider your customer's budget. All brands can be broadly categorised into three price levels: house brands, premium brands and super/ultra premium.

Flavoured vodka
42 Below: Feijoa (pineapple/guava), Kiwi, Manuka honey and Passion Fruit.
Absolut: Apeach, Citron, Kurant, Mandrin, Mango, Pears, Peppar, Raspberri, Ruby Red and Vanilia.
Belvedere: Cytrus and Pomeranca.
Finlandia: Cranberry, Grapefruit, Lime and Mango.
Grey Goose: L'Orange, Le Citron and La Poire.

Wyborowa: Dzika Rose, Rajskie Apple, Klapsa Pear, Swieza Lemon and Almond
Zubrowka: Bison, with notes of vanilla.

GRAIN DISTILLATES: GIN

Famous for the classic Martini and the quintessential English serve G&T, the category of gin has experienced a shake-up in recent years with the addition of some notable brands. Although some may argue that gin is simply flavoured vodka, the category offers a wide and varied selection of individual spirits and some unique production methods.

ORIGINS

Reports from Amsterdam's excise records confirm that juniper cordials and elixirs were being drunk and widely exported during the 15th century, with unrefined grain spirit being combined with juniper and sugar to disguise the volatile impurities of early spirit production. Gin was originally called 'genever', taken from the French word genièvre, meaning juniper. This became very popular and found its way to the UK through the British soldiers fighting in Holland and the name was shortened to gin and referred to as 'Holland's' or 'Dutch courage'.

Gin's early popularity grew when William of Orange became King of England in 1689 (King William III) and declared war on the French. He reinforced this by banning all French imports, which included brandies and wines. Subsequently a law was passed in 1690 encouraging distillation in England that meant anybody could distil grain spirit for a very low tax. In turn this spawned what was known as the gin craze and by the early 1730s there were believed to be several thousand back-street distilleries, run from people's homes, all attempting to make gin.

To date, the majority of quality gin is mainly produced in the United Kingdom, although international brands such as South Gin and Junipero have recently come on the market. The introduction in recent years of brands such as Blackwoods, Millers and Hendricks means a broader range of gins is now available.

PRODUCTION

Gin is a clear, un-aged vodka-like grain spirit. It is possible to use molasses instead of grain as the base and some believe this gives the gin a sweeter edge. Gin is a spirit with an ABV of over 37.5%. The initial production process of a rectified spirit is similar to that of vodka and can be made using both continuous and/or pot still distillation. Gin is then redistilled with botanicals.

Most gins contain a high proportion of juniper and coriander but, there are over one hundred different botanicals used in the production of gin and it is the combination of these that give each brand its own unique character. Here are some of the most popular botanicals used in modern gin production.

Almonds: nutty, bitter oil extracted from the almond fruit.
Angelica: root botanical of the parsley family.
Aniseed: liquorice-flavoured seed.
Caraway: aniseed-flavoured spice.
Cardamom: aromatic spicy black seeds.
Cassia bark: oil extracted from the bark with a bitter cinnamon flavour.
Cinnamon: aromatic spice native to Sri Lanka and South India; the seeds are used to flavour gin.

Citrus peel: including lemon, lime, orange and grapefruit. Dried out skins and oils of citrus fruits are used to flavour the spirit.
Coriander: the second most popular botanical used to make gin, it gives spicy, floral notes.
Cubeb berries: pine and lemon flavour berries with a peppery spice.
Fennel: aniseed flavoured seed.
Ginger: fiery spicy root
Grains of paradise: dark brown nut that adds floral spicy notes.
Juniper: the juniper berry is the most commonly used botanical to flavour gin. Its bittersweet floral oils add a delicate aroma to gin.
Lavender: distinctive floral aromas from this pale purple plant.

Liquorice: a bittersweet botanical with distinctive sweet herbal flavours.
Nutmeg: sweet, nutty spice.
Orris: fragrant floral root that binds the flavours in gin.

The botanical mix and how its flavours are imparted into the spirit varies with each producer. Beefeater steep their botanicals in the base spirit for 24 hours before distillation; Gordon's and Tanqueray use a two-shot method, adding the botanicals to neutral spirit and water in a copper pot still and gently apply heat until boiling, producing a highly concentrated flavour. Neutral spirit is then added after distillation. Bombay Sapphire, on the other hand, have an

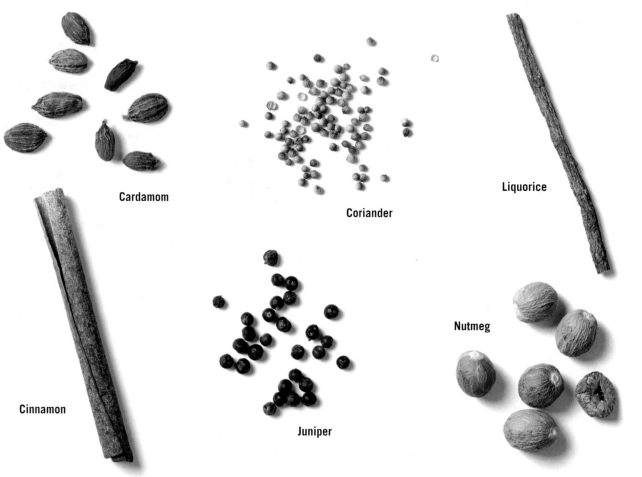

Cardamom

Coriander

Liquorice

Nutmeg

Cinnamon

Juniper

altogether unique method of imparting the flavours of their botanical mix, whereby the vapours from distillation pass through a tray of botanicals, also known as steaming.

Reducing the spirit to bottling strength works in the same way as with other spirits, by adding water after distillation. It is also worth noting the range of bottling strengths of gin, which varies from 37.5 to 57% ABV.

BRANDS

Just like other spirits, all brands can be broadly categorised into three price levels: house brands, premium brands and super/ultra premium.

Flavoured gin
Bramley & Gage Damson Gin (UK)
Gordon Sloe Gin (UK)
Plymouth Sloe Gin (UK)
Hendricks Cucumber Gin (Scotland)

ESSENTIAL SERVES

Gin's perfect partner is tonic, and this is the most popular combination, certainly in the UK and for the British clientele. Gin and orange juice is also a popular international bar call, along with gin and it, 'it' being Italian sweet red vermouth.

Classic cocktails that call for gin are the classic Dry Martini, Red Snapper, Gin Sour, Gin Sling, Gimlet, Gin Fix, Gin Fizz and the Tom Collins. A popular contemporary cocktail comes in the form of the Bramble, created by the legendary Dick Bradsell, and on menus the world over.

HOUSE BRANDS
Beefeater (UK)
Bombay Sapphire (UK)
Broker's (UK)
Cork (Ireland)
Finsbury's (UK)
Gilbey's (US)
Gloags (UK)
Gordon's (UK)
Greenalls (UK)
Larios (Spain)
Plymouth (UK)
Seagram's Extra Dry (US)

PREMIUM BRANDS
No 209 Gin (US)
Blackwood's (Scotland)
Bulldog Gin (UK)
Citadelle (France)
Daresbury's
  Quintessential (UK)
Millers (UK)
Plymouth Navy (UK)
Tanqueray (London, UK)
Whitley Neill (UK)

SUPER/ULTRA PREMIUM
Junipero (US)
Right Gin (Sweden)
South Gin (New Zealand)
Tanqueray 10 (UK)

DISTILLED KNOWLEDGE ABOUT GIN
- The word 'gin' is an abbreviation of the Dutch word 'genever', meaning juniper
- There are five categories of gin: London Dry, Plymouth, Old Tom, Genever and flavoured gin.
- Gin must be un-aged, colourless and unsweetened
- Gin is made by redistilling a base spirit with natural botanical
- The predominant flavour in gin is juniper berries
- Coriander is the second most used botanical
- Gin is distilled to 96% ABV before reducing to bottling strength. It has to have a minimum of 37.5% ABV in the EC to be classed as a gin.

GRAIN DISTILLATES: WHISKY

The word whisky comes from the Celtic word meaning 'water of life'. The subtleties of this dark spirit can be a minefield to the uneducated bartender, so this section will illustrate the different styles of whisky and give the modern bartender an insight into the production of this highly complex spirit.

ORIGINS

It is generally accepted that whisky originated in Ireland although the Scottish will argue this. Whisky was being made in Ireland by the 12th century, although some claim a type of whisky was being made by monks as early as the 6th century. From here it spread to Scotland and later to the US and beyond.

PRODUCTION

Whisky is an aged, grain spirit. It is made in many countries around the world, each using different production methods and techniques that define the characteristics of that country's particular style of whisky.

To make whisky you must first harvest the grain, which is softened with the addition of moisture. The grain is then roasted, cooked or baked dry and ground into a coarse flour called the 'grist'. Water and yeast are added to make the 'wort', which is fermented for two to three days and is then known as the 'wash', an alcoholic 'beer' around 6–8% ABV. This wash is then distilled once to around 21–30% ABV and the resulting liquid is called a 'low wine'. It is distilled again to around 60% ABV and can go on to be made into whiskey. Once that process is over it must then be aged in wooden barrels to add flavour and colour to the clear, raw whisky. Most whiskies are aged in oak but it depends on the individual whisky being made as to which wood is used and how long it is aged.

STYLES

Whiskies are generally categorised into the following headings: malt, grain and blended, Irish, American, Canadian and Japanese.

Scottish malt whisky

To be called Scotch whisky the spirit must conform to the standards of the Scotch Whisky Order of 1990 (UK). There are two major definitions: single and blended. Single means that the product is from a single distillery; blended means that the product is composed of whiskies from two or more distilleries.

Single malt whisky is a 100% malted barley whisky from one distillery.

Single grain whisky is a grain whisky from one distillery (it does not have to be made from a single type of grain it can be from a mixture of cereals).

Vatted, pure or **blended malt whisky** is a malt whisky created by mixing single malt whiskies from more than one distillery.

Blended grain whisky is a whisky created by mixing grain whiskies from more than one distillery.

SINGLE MALT SCOTCH MEANS:
Single: whisky from one distillery only.
Malt: only barley must be malted (allowed to part-germinate).
Scotch: legally Scotch whisky must be aged in Scotland for a minimum of three years.

Blended Scotch whisky is a mixture of single malt whisky and grain whisky, usually from multiple distilleries.

PRODUCTION

The grain used in malt whisky must be barley and only barley. Once harvested the barley is then malted. This means soaked in water for one or two days and allowed to part-germinate. After soaking, the grain is spread out on to the floor and constantly turned to dry it out and prepare it for peat smoking.

To stop all the sugars being absorbed by the barley it is dried in a kiln. Scotch whisky traditionally uses peat fires, and the smoke from the fire passes through the drying barley, which imparts Scotch's characteristic smoky flavour. The barley is then ground down into a powder called 'grist' and mixed with warm water in a 'mash-tun', turning the starch in the barley into simple sugars; the resulting solution is known as 'wort'. The wort is then transferred to large vats and yeast is added, starting the fermentation process. This process takes between 48 and 60 hours and creates the 'wash', which ranges between 7–9% alcohol. The fermented wash must then be distilled twice, usually using pot stills; some scotches, however, are triple distilled.

The first distillation produces the 'low wines', which are usually around 21%–30% ABV. This liquid is then distilled a second time in a smaller pot still. It is at this stage that the master distiller must carefully separate the middle runnings, also known as 'heart', of the distillation, which is considered the best part of

the distillation. This creates a distillate of approximately 70% ABV. The first and last runnings, also known as the 'heads' or 'foreshots' and 'tails' or 'feints', are cut and added back into the low wines for re-distillation.

The spirit leaves the still clear and is then diluted, with water, to around 60–63% ABV and added to oak casks for a minimum of three years by law, although the malt whiskies are generally aged for eight to 12 years. Some malt whiskies reach their peak around this age, however, others can reach their peak from 15 to 30 years and older, in some cases 50 years. Sherry and ex-bourbon barrels are mainly used in the maturation of Scotch malt whisky, giving their own character to the final product. You will also find some whiskies are finished, for a period of six to 12 months, in port barrels.

Maturation further reduces the alcohol content to around 48–62% ABV. Unless this is then bottled at 'cask strength' it is then watered down one last time to a minimum bottling strength of 40% ABV.

MALT WHISKY REGIONS
There are over 100 distilleries in Scotland, separated by their geographical locations into six regions, each giving their own unique style.

THE HIGHLANDS
The Highlands is the largest of the whisky producing areas of Scotland and has a number of different variations in styles. From the coastal whiskies from the western areas that give a salty and peaty character to

the more northern which produce a spicier character, with the eastern and southern parts of the Highlands producing a fruitier style.

Highland whiskies include:
Aberfeldy 12 Year Old (40% ABV)
Balblair 12 Year Old (40% ABV)
Ben Nevis 12 Year Old (46% ABV)
Blair Athol 12 Year Old (43% ABV)
Clynelish 12 to 14 Year Old (40–43% ABV)
Dalwhinnie 15 Year Old (43% ABV)
Deanston 12 Year Old (40% ABV)
Edradour 10 Year Old (40% ABV)
Glengoyne 17 Year Old (43% ABV)
Glenmorangie 10 to 30 Year Old (40–44.3% ABV)
Glen Ord 12 Year Old (40% ABV)
Oban 12 Year Old (43% ABV)

SPEYSIDE
Speyside is a sub-region of the Highlands and acknowledged as the heart of Scotch whisky production. The whiskies from this region are noted for their floral heather-honey notes and peatiness.

Speyside whiskies include:
Aberlour 10 Year Old (40% ABV)
Aultmore 12 Year Old (40% ABV)
Balvenie 10 to 25 Year Old (40–50.4% ABV)

Cardhu 12 Year Old (40% ABV)
Cardhu 1973, 27 Year Old (60.25% ABV)
Cragganmore 12 Year Old (40% ABV)
Dalmore 12 to 21 Year Old (40% ABV)
Glenfarclas 10 to 15 Year Old (40–46% ABV)
Glenfiddich 12, 70 Year Old (40–44% ABV)
Glen Grant 10 to 25 Year Old (40–56% ABV)
The Glenlivet 12 to 30 Year Old (40–48% ABV)
Knockando 12 Year Old (43% ABV)
Linkwood 12 Year Old (43% ABV)
The Macallan 10 to 25 Year Old (40–43% ABV)
Mannochmore 12 Year Old (43% ABV)
The Singleton 10 Year Old (40% ABV)
The Strathisla 12 Year Old (40% ABV)
Tamdhu 10 Year Old (40% ABV)

THE ISLANDS
The Islands include the Orkney Isles, the Isle of Jura, the Isle of Skye, the Isle of Mull and the Isle of Arran. These whiskies tend to be more rounded, dry and have a distinct peatiness.

The Islands whiskies include:
Arran 10 Year Old (43% ABV)
Highland Park 12 to 25 Year Old (40–53.5% ABV)
Jura 10 to 30 Year Old (40–55.5% ABV)
Talisker 10 to 25 Year Old (40–62% ABV)
Tobermoray 10 Year Old (43% ABV)

CAMPBELTOWN

A town on the Mull of Kintyre produces briny, salty whiskies and has only two distilleries, Springbank and Glen Scotia.

Campbeltown whiskies include:
Glen Scotia 1991 MacPhails Collection (40% ABV)
Springbank 10 Year Old (46% ABV)

ISLAY

The island has seven distilleries that produce sea-like, peaty, sometimes medicinal flavours.

Islay whiskies include:
Ardbeg 10 Year Old (46% ABV)
Ardbeg 17 Year Old (40% ABV)
Bowmore 12 Year Old (40% ABV)
Bowmore 12 to 25 Year Old (40–43% ABV)
Bruichladdich 10 to 20 Year Old (43–46% ABV)
Bunnahabhain 12 Year Old (40% ABV)
Bunnahabhain 1965 35 Year Old (53.9% ABV)
Caol ila 12 to 23 Year Old (40–61.7% ABV)
Lagavulin 16 Year Old (40% ABV)
Lagavulin 25 Year Old (57.2% ABV)
Laphroaig 10 Year Old (43% ABV)
Laphroaig 15 Year Old (43% ABV)
Laphroaig 30 Year Old (43% ABV)

THE LOWLANDS

The Lowlands is the south region of Scotland and produces soft and grassy malts.

Lowland whiskies include:
Auchentoshan 10 Year Old (40% ABV)
Auchentoshan 21 Year Old (43% ABV)
Bladnoch 10 to 23 Year Old (40–55% ABV)
Glenkinchie 10 Year Old (43% ABV)
Rosebank 12 Year Old (43% ABV)
Rosebank 20 Year Old (57% ABV)

ESSENTIAL SERVES

Malts have become quite popular as a base in certain classic cocktails such as the Old Fashioned and Manhattan, although hardened malt whisky traditionalists would insist on serving malt whiskies neat or with water at room temperature.

Scottish grain and blended whisky (Scotch) history

It is widely accepted that in 1860, the Spirits Act made it legal to blend whiskies from different distilleries, and Andrew Usher & Co began using grain whiskies to blend with traditional malts, producing a lighter whiskey that appealed to a larger market.

PRODUCTION

Scotch is a blend of distilled malt and grain whiskies. It must be made in Scotland from grain grown in Scotland and aged for a minimum of three years in Scotland and bottled at a minimum of 40% ABV.

ESSENTIAL SERVES

Blended Scotch whisky is enjoyed with many different carbonated mixers, most popularly Coca Cola and ginger ale. Scotch is used in many classic cocktails including the Rob Roy, Scotch Sour and Sandy Collins.

Irish whiskey

It is believed that Ireland was the birthplace of whiskey and it has a similar history to that of Scotch insofar as distilling was noted to be practised from around the 12th century, with its consumption widespread throughout the 16th century. Irish whiskey has had a chequered past, most notably in the form of a trade embargo which banned trade to any of the countries within the British Empire and the banning of distillation during the second world war. Today though, Irish whiskey has enjoyed a resurgence and is the fastest growing whiskey category.

PRODUCTION

Irish whiskey can be made from any grain, using malted barley, unmalted and other cereals in the mash bill. Irish whiskies are made in a similar way to Scotch, however, in general the grain is not peat smoked.

Irish whiskies generally also use a combination of column and pot distillation and by law should be distilled a minimum of three times. Grain whiskies are generally continuously distilled whereas malt whiskies use pot distillation. Once the spirit has left the distillation it must be aged for a minimum of three years in oak casks in Ireland, usually in ex-sherry, bourbon and rum barrels, to be classified as an Irish whiskey.

The final part of production is the vatting process, also referred to as blending. At this stage the different grain and malt whiskies are placed in large vats and left to marry for a period of two days to one month.

BRANDS

There are only three distilleries operating in Ireland: Midleton, Bushmills and Cooley's. They each make a range of brands which include:

Black Bush (40% ABV)
Bushmills Original (40% ABV)
Inishowen (40% ABV)
Jameson (40% ABV)
Kilbeggan (40% ABV)
Locke's Blend (40% ABV)
Midleton Very Rare (40% ABV)
Millars (40% ABV)
Powers (40% ABV)
Paddy (40% ABV)
Tullamore Dew (40% ABV)

ESSENTIAL SERVES

Irish whiskey is enjoyed with a little water or over ice and with many carbonated mixers, most popularly with ginger ale. Irish whiskey is used in cocktails such as the Irish Coffee and as a substitute for Scotch in some cocktails.

American whiskey

Grain distillates first started being made towards the late 18th century when Thomas Jefferson offered plots of land to pioneer settlers. Most of the early settlers were Scottish or Irish immigrants escaping famine, bringing the production methods and techniques from their forefathers and growing copious amounts of corn.

It is believed that Reverend Elijah Craig made the first true bourbon whiskey and was credited to have invented the charred barrel method of ageing the whiskey. Legend has it that he purchased a barrel that had previously been used to store fish and burnt the inside of the barrel to remove the smell before he put his whiskey in it to transport it down river to New Orleans for sale. The barrels had been stamped in the port of Mayville, Bourbon County, and so the name bourbon was born. However,

others credit Dr James Crow as the father of bourbon who created and perfected the sour mash technique between 1825 and 1845.

BOURBON PRODUCTION

American whiskey is produced in similar ways to Irish and Scotch whiskies although there are some very distinguishing features and methods. Starting with the grain, predominantly more corn and rye are used than barley. By law, Bourbon can be made anywhere in the USA, but it is mainly native to the Southern state of Kentucky. Only Bourbon from Kentucky can advertise the state in which it is made (Kentucky Straight Bourbon Whiskey). It must contain at least 51% corn but no more than 80% with the other 20–49% comprising of a combination of rye, barley and wheat.

The mash bill is pressure cooked with water, generally limestone water, and yeast is then added. A signature of American whiskey is the addition of the 'sour mash' which is around 25% of the mash from the previous whiskey batches which is then added to the fermentation, helping to maintain a consistent style. This sour mash is then fermented into beer and distilled, always twice and on occasion more. Different brands and styles use a combination of pot and continuous distillation and some brands only use pot stills to a strength of around 63% ABV.

All straight American whiskies, except straight corn whiskey, must be aged in new American white oak casks that have been charred on their inside surface for a minimum of two years. The charring of the wood

caramelises the sap and imparts sweet and smoky flavours to the whiskey during ageing. The barrels cannot be re-used in Bourbon, so they are sold on to other spirit distillers of Scotch, tequila and rum.

The spirit is then reduced with water to bottling strength between 40–62.5% ABV by law.

TENNESSEE WHISKEY PRODUCTION

The main difference between Bourbon and Tennessee whiskey is the Lincoln County Process by which the whiskey is filtered through maple charcoal before ageing. Tennessee whiskey must be made of at least 51% of a single grain and can only be made in Tennessee.

CORN WHISKEY PRODUCTION

An American whiskey containing more than 51% corn and aged in old barrels is called a corn whiskey.

RYE WHISKEY PRODUCTION

A whiskey made with at least 51% rye in its mash bill but with other grains including a significant amount of corn. There is no minimum ageing period, however, to be called 'straight rye' it must be aged for at least two years in new oak barrels.

BRANDS

Bakers (53.5% ABV)
Basil Hayden's 8 Year Old (40% ABV)
Blanton's – various ages and strength
Booker's – 6–8 Years Old
   (60.5–62.5% ABV)
Buffalo Trace (45% ABV)
Bulleit (45% ABV)
Eagle Rare (50.5% ABV)
Elijah Craig 12 Year Old (47% ABV)

Evan Williams 23 Year Old (53.5% ABV)
Fighting Cock (51.5% ABV)
Four Roses (40% ABV)
Gentleman Jack (40% ABV)
Jack Daniel's Old No.7 Brand (40% ABV)
Jack Daniel's Single Barrel (47% ABV)
Jim Beam Black Label (43% ABV)
Jim Beam White Label (40% ABV)
Johnny Drum 12 Year Old (43% ABV)
Knob Creek (50% ABV)

Maker's Mark (45% ABV)
Old Potrero Straight Rye (62.1% ABV)
Old Rip Van Winkle 10 Year Old
   (45% ABV)
Old Rip Van Winkle 15 Years Old
   (53.5% ABV)
Rittenhouse Straight Rye (40% ABV)
Wild Turkey (50.5% ABV)
Woodford Reserve (45.2% ABV)

ESSENTIAL SERVES

Historically a sipping spirit served neat or over ice, but made popular by the bar call of 'JD and Coke'. Popular classic cocktails that use Bourbon are the legendary Old Fashioned and some other notable classics such as Sazerac, Manhattan, Sours and the Mint Julep.

Canadian whisky

Whisky was first introduced to Canada by John Molson (better known for Molson beer) in 1799 and centered around the town of Kingston, Lake Ontario, and spread as farming developed. The first legal Canadian whisky distillery was founded in 1832, and in 1875 the Canadian government created regulations that stated it must be made from cereals grown in Canada and use continuous distillation. The law also states that Canadian whisky must be aged for a minimum of three years and a maximum of 18 years in charred oak barrels.

PRODUCTION

It is the flexibility of Canadian whisky regulations that allows for many different styles. The producers can have greatly varied mashbills, different still sizes and can age in woods from Jerez, Scotland, Bourbon or Porto. The whisky is usually aged, blended and then married in casks for a period after blending.

BRANDS

Black Velvet (40% ABV)
Canadian Club (40% ABV)
Canadian Mist (40% ABV)
Crown Royal (40% ABV)
Forty Creek (40% ABV)

ESSENTIAL SERVES

Similar to other whiskies served neat or over ice, but great served with cola, lemonade or ginger ale as a tall drink. A classic cocktail that makes good use of Canadian whisky is the Manhattan.

Japanese whisky

Although the Japanese whisky industry is a relatively new one it has the largest whisky distillery in the world, at Suntory near Kyoto, with 24 pot stills. Japanese whisky was developed in the 1920s by two men, Masataka Taketsuru and Shinjiro Torii. Masataka went to Scotland in 1918 and studied Applied Chemistry at Glasgow University while spending time working in the Scotch whisky distilleries. Shinjiro provided the finance to open the Suntory distillery, and the first brand, Shirofuda, was launched in 1929. A second brand, Kakubin, was launched in 1937 and still sells to this date.

PRODUCTION

Japanese whisky is made in a very similar way to Scotch but is a lighter style that better suits Japanese cuisine.

BRANDS

Hibiki (43% ABV)
Kakubin (43% ABV)
Nikka Miyagikyo 10 Year Old
   (45% ABV)
Royal Whisky (43% ABV)
Yamazaki (43% ABV)

ESSENTIAL SERVES

Generally served neat or over ice or with a little water.

PLANT DISTILLATES:

Plant distillates are identified by the following broad spirit categories of rum (molasses), cachaça (sugar cane juice), tequila and mezcal (agave).

RUM

In the English colonies rum was called 'kill devil' or 'rumbullion', which was shortened over the years to rum. This category is made famous by the worldwide dominance of Bacardi and in recent times has seen dozens of smaller distillers distributing their finely crafted brands across the globe, creating a plethora of choice for the consumer and bartender. The following reveals an interesting past and highlights the production methods and most notable brands.

ORIGINS

It is not entirely clear who invented rum or when it was first distilled, however the origins of rum are found in the production of sugar, from sugar cane. It is believed that the development of fermented drinks produced from sugar cane juice was first discovered in ancient India or China, and subsequently spread from there. One of the earliest recordings was in the 14th century by Marco Polo who was offered a 'very good wine of sugar'. It is also believed that it was Christopher Columbus who first planted sugar cane in the West Indies on his second voyage to the Americas in 1493. Sugar cane was then widely planted throughout the Caribbean and used as a commodity, whilst the use of molasses, the syrupy liquid resulting from the refining of sugar cane, remained undiscovered.

It is accepted that by the 1650s sugar mill operators soon noticed that when molasses were mixed with water and left out in the sun they would ferment into an unrefined version of what we now know as rum. Rum was then used as a cure-all for many of the aches and pains that afflicted those living in the tropics and sugar plantation owners sold it to naval ships that were on station in the Caribbean.

After rum's development in the Caribbean, the drink's popularity spread into Colonial America and to support this demand the first rum distillery was set up in 1664 on Staten Island. With demand high, rum joined gold as an accepted currency in Europe for a period of time and to further support this demand for the molasses to produce rum, a labour source to work the sugar plantations in the Caribbean was needed.

The shipping of molasses to New England distilleries became part of the infamous 'slavery triangle'. The first leg was the shipment of molasses to New England to make rum. The second leg was the shipment of rum to the ports of West

Africa to trade for slaves. The final leg was the passage of slave ships to the sugar plantations of the Caribbean and South America where many of the slaves were put to work in the sugar cane fields.

The disruption of trade caused by the American Revolution, in the latter part of the 18th century, and the rise of whiskey production in North America resulted in the slow decline of rum's dominance as the American national tipple. Rum production in the United States slowly decreased through the 19th century, with the last New England rum distilleries closing at the advent of Prohibition in 1920.

Until the second half of the 19th century all rums were heavy or dark rums that were considered appropriate for the working poor and in order to expand the market for rum, the Spanish Royal Development Board offered a prize to anyone who could improve the rum-making process. One of the most important figures in this development process was Don Facundo Bacardi Masso, who moved from Spain to Santiago de Cuba in 1843. Don Facundo's experiments with distillation techniques, charcoal filtering, cultivating of specialised yeast strains, and ageing with American oak casks helped to produce a smoother, mellower drink typical of modern light rums. It was with this new rum that Don Facundo founded Bacardí y Compañía in 1862, and as they say, the rest is history.

PRODUCTION

Rum is produced around the world, however, the main region for rum production is the Caribbean. Sugar cane is where rum production begins. Once the cane is harvested it is passed through a series of rollers and grinders that squeeze the juice out from the stems. The juice is then heated and clarified before being pumped into evaporators that drive off any excess water. The liquid is then cool-boiled in a vacuum to create a syrupy mixture from which sugar crystals are extracted. The treacle-like liquid that remains is known as molasses.

Rums are made either from sugar cane juice or molasses. The sugar cane juice or molasses is then fermented from 12 hours up to 12 days, creating a light or a heavier style respectively. Cane juice can be fermented without adding any water, as its sugar content is naturally low enough. After fermentation, the wash is approximately 5–9% ABV.

The wash is then distilled by using either a pot or column still, or in some cases both methods, to approximately 85% ABV. Pot still rums tend to produce heavier rums and column-distilled rums tend to be lighter and cleaner.

The next stage in rum's production is maturation. Before the rum is placed in barrels it is often reduced with water to around 80% ABV. The majority of barrels used in the Caribbean are ex-Bourbon and Jack Daniels barrels and are sometimes re-charred on the inside to help impart more of the character from the wood, as well as to re-caramelize the sugars in the wood.

It is estimated that Caribbean rum matures at approximately three times the rate of Scotch or Cognac; this is due to the climate and temperature of the region. Therefore, tropical ageing may mean that a six-year-old rum may have the same qualities as an 18-year-old Scotch. Even white rums will be aged for up to three years; the colour is then filtered out using charcoal.

Most rums are then blended with different ages and styles to create the distillery's own unique style. At this stage some add caramel to ensure a consistency of colour and in some cases, to help give a sweeter, more caramelised taste and aroma. The rum is then allowed to 'marry' in vats before it is reduced with water to bottling strength.

RUM STYLES

Although there is no legal definition for the classification of rums they can be divided as follows:

White (blanco, light or silver): this is the clear white rum famed by Bacardi, which is light bodied and charcoal filtered.

Gold (oro): this is slightly sweeter rum with the taste often coming from the addition of caramel and/or wood ageing.

Aged (añejo/rhum vieux): aged rums are gaining new standing among consumers of single malt Scotch whiskies, Armagnacs, and small-batch Bourbons who are learning to appreciate the subtle complexities of these rums. The pot still rums of St Lucia, Guyana and Jamaica have a particular appeal for Scotch whisky drinkers.

Single barrel: this rum is taken from individual barrels and generally bottled as a vintage.

Overproof: usually very strong, clear and over 57% ABV.

Dark (navy or black): caramel is often added for colour and flavour and usually bottled at a higher percentage.

BRANDS

There are literally hundreds of different brands, with several coming from the same distillery. Here is a sample of some popular and more unique rums on the market that are worth knowing. Age statements are approximate as tropical ageing conditions must be taken into consideration.

Angostura (Trinidad)
Angostura white rum (37.5% ABV)
Angostura 5 Year Old (40% ABV)
Angostura 7 Year Old (40% ABV)
Angostura 1919, 8 Year Old (40% ABV)
Angostura 1824, 12 Year Old
    (40% ABV)

Appleton Estate & J Wray & Nephew (Jamaica)
Appleton Estate Extra 12 to 18 Year
    Old (40% ABV)
Appleton Special (40% ABV)
Appleton V/X 5 to 10 Year Old
    (40% ABV)
Appleton White (40% ABV)

Appleton 21 Year Old (43% ABV)
Wray & Nephew Overproof
  (63% ABV)

Bacardi (worldwide)
Bacardi Carta Blanca (37.5% ABV)
Bacardi Oro (37.5% ABV)
Bacardi 8 Year Old (40.5% ABV)

J Bally (Martinique)
J Bally Blanc (50% ABV)
J Bally Ambre (45% ABV)
J Bally Martinique 1987 (45% ABV)

Barbancourt (Haiti)
Barbancourt Three Star 4 Year Old
(43% ABV)
Barbancourt Five Star 8 Year Old
(43% ABV)
Barbancourt Estate Reserve 15 Year
Old (43% ABV)

Bundaberg (Australia)
Bundaberg OP (57.7% ABV)
Bundaberg UP (37% ABV)

Captain Morgan (originally Jamaica)
Captain Morgan Black Label
  (40% ABV)
Captain Morgan's Original Spiced
  (40% ABV)

Clement (Martinique)
Clement Blanc (40-50% ABV)
Clement Canne Bleue (50% ABV)
Clement Grappe Blanche (50% ABV)
Clement VSOP (40% ABV)
Clement XO (44% ABV)

Cockspur (Barbados)
Cockspur Old Gold (43% ABV)
Cockspur Rum (37.5% ABV)
Cockspur VSOR (43% ABV)

El Dorado/Demerara Distillers (Guyana)
El Dorado 5 Year Old (40% ABV)
El Dorado Demerara Spice (40% ABV)

Gosling's (Bermuda)
Gosling's Black Seal (40% ABV)
Gosling's Gold (40% ABV)

Havana Club (Cuba)
Havana Club Silver Dry (40% ABV)
Havana Club 3 Year Old (40% ABV)
Havana Club Añejo Reserva 5 Year
  Old (40% ABV)
Havana Club 7 Year Old (40% ABV)
Havana Club Extra Aged 15 Year Old
  (40% ABV)

Lamb's Navy Rum (worldwide)
  (40% ABV)

Matasulem (Dominican Republic)
Matasulem Clasico 10 Year Old
  (40% ABV)
Matasulem Gran Reserva 15 Year
Old (40% ABV)
Matasulem Platino (40% ABV)

Mount Gay (Barbados)
Mount Gay Eclipse (40% ABV)
Mount Gay XO (40% ABV)

Myers's (Jamaica) (40% ABV)

Pampero (Venezuela) (40% ABV)

Pirassununga 51 (Brazil) (40% ABV)

Pusser's Rum (US) (54.5% ABV)

Ron Zacapa Centenario (Guatemala)
  (40% ABV)

St Lucia Distillers (St Lucia)
Admiral Rodney (40% ABV)
Bounty Rum (40% ABV)

Chairman's Reserve (40% ABV)
TØZ Rum (40% ABV)

Wood's 100 Old Navy (Guyana)
  (57% ABV)

ESSENTIAL SERVES

Rum and coconut water is the
most popular Caribbean mix, made
locally with fresh coconuts, but
internationally rum is served
primarily with cola and a wedge
of fresh lime (Cuba Libre). Other
popular long drinks include rum and
ginger ale, and mixed drinks include
the Pina Colada, Mojito and tiki
drinks such as the Zombie or Mai
Tai.

Aged rums should be savoured
either for sipping on the rocks or
with a classic cocktail, liberating the
unique flavours in such concoctions
as the Daiquiri and the Añejo Old
Fashioned.

DISTILLED KNOWLEDGE ABOUT RUM
- Rum is a plant distillate
- Rum is made from fermented sugar
  cane juice or from molasses, created
  as a by-product of sugar making.
- It takes approximately 1.5 gallons of
  molasses to make 1 gallon of rum
- Rum is distilled a minimum of two
  times
- Distilled to between 60–96% ABV
  before reducing to bottling strength
- Must be a minimum of 37.5% ABV
  in the EU to be classed as rum
- Rum can be aged, un-aged,
  flavoured and dark

CACHAÇA

Pronounced ka-sha-sa, this rum-like spirit has been produced for centuries in Brazil and has recently found its way around the world, mainly in the form of a Caipirinha. Cachaça is recognised as the spirit of Brazil and is made from sugar cane juice, also known as rum agricole, caninha, meaning little water, and aguardente de cana.

There are two types of cachaça production: artisanal, mainly used by the thousands of small independent producers in their own copper pot stills, and industrial, used by a small number of large distilleries who generally used continuous distillation.

There are a number of notable differences between rum production and cachaça. Cachaça is made from sugar cane juice and distilled up to 75% ABV, which gives it its raw edge. Also, according to the drinks laws of Brazil, it must be bottled between 38–54%. Cachaça must age for a minimum of one year and use different types of native and exotic wood for its casks, including chestnut, balsam, brazil wood, cherry, umburana and more commonly oak.

CACHAÇA TYPES

Some cachaças have age statements and are generally classified by the following terms:

Pura (crystal): unaged
Velho: the spirit has been aged for a minimum of one year

BRANDS

Beija-Flor Pura (39% ABV)
Beija-Flor Velho (39% ABV)
Beija-Flor 10 Year Old (39% ABV)
Brasilla (40% ABV)
Germana Single Barrel (40% ABV)
Germana 2 Year Old (41.6% ABV)
Germana 10 Year Old (43% ABV)
Pirassununga 51 Cachaça
 (40% ABV)
Pitu (40% ABV)
Sagatiba Pura (38% ABV)
Sagatiba Velho (40% ABV)
Velho Barreiro (40% ABV)
Ypioca Crystal (39% ABV)
Ypioca Gold (39% ABV)

ESSENTIAL SERVES

Bombeirinho is a local drink made with cachaça and red gooseberry syrup. The most popular way of serving cachaça is in the Caipirinha, using fresh lime and sugar. Aged cachaça can be sipped on the rocks or used in a Cachaça Daiquiri or Velho Old Fashioned and can also be used as the base in a Mojito.

DISTILLED KNOWLEDGE ABOUT CACHAÇA

- Cachaça is also known as rum agricole, caninha, meaning little water, and aguardente de cana.
- Aged (velho) Cachaça must spend a minimum of one year in the cask.
- According to the drinks laws of Brazil, it must be bottled between 38–54%.
- There are approximately 30,000 cachaça manufacturers producing 5,000 different brands of the spirit.
- Pirassununga 51 Cachaça is the largest producer and sells around a third of all cachaça in Brazil.
- Germany has become one of the largest consumers of cachaça outside Latin America. Paraguay is the largest importer and consumer outside of Brazil.

TEQUILA AND MEZCAL

The origins of tequila date back to 250–300 AD, when Aztecs first fermented the juice from the heart of agave plants to make a wine, referred to as 'pulque' or 'agua miel'.

Over time the techniques of tequila production have improved and modernised with new laws governing the production and labelling of tequila, protecting the national spirit of Mexico. Those distilleries that adhere to the production regulations are given a NOM number (Norma Oficial Mexicana de Calidad), which is printed on each bottle. All brands of 100% blue agave tequila will have a NOM on the label, however, this is not a guarantee of quality, only of authenticity.

TEQUILA PRODUCTION

The raw ingredient used in the production of tequila is taken from the blue agave, however, mezcal can be made using any type of agave plant, of which there are over 200 types. The agave is a member of the lily (amaryllis) family and is often mistaken for a cactus.

Firstly the hearts of the agave, which look a lot like giant pineapples and weigh between 30 and 90 kg (70 and 200 lb), are harvested by hand. They are then cooked in an autoclave for 8–14 hours or in a steam oven for 72 hours. The hearts are then left to cool for about 24 hours in a traditional stone mill called a Chilean mill and then pressed to extract the sugary sap (known as agua miel) and mixed with water

to form the basis for fermentation.

Similarly to the sour mash fermentation of bourbon, juice from the previous batch is mixed in to give a consistency of flavour, which takes between 36 and 72 hours. This results in the beer, known as 'mosto', which has an approximate ABV of 5–7%. The 'mosto' has to be distilled a minimum of two times to be classified as tequila, generally in copper pot stills, and only a handful of distillers distill a third time.

If the pure distillate is then used to make tequila it is referred to as 100% agave, or this distillate can be blended with other raw spirits, most often from sugar cane, to produce 'mixto' tequila. At this stage the spirit can be reduced with water to a minimum of 38% ABV and then bottled, producing a blanco or silver tequila.

Other than the percentage of agave spirit used, tequila is also categorised according to the length of time it has spent in a cask, of which the most popular type used is old bourbon casks. Reposado (meaning rested) and añejo (aged) tequilas are aged for 60 days to one year, and upwards of one year respectively, mellowing and imparting some of the aged notes found in some whiskies. Some producers then bottle the liquid straight from the cask, but more often water is added to reduce it to

bottling strength, which is generally around 38–40% ABV.

As with cognac, tequila by law can only originate from within five designated regions of Mexico (their ruling is not dissimilar to that of the French appellation contrôlée).

MEZCAL PRODUCTION

There are a number of differences between tequila and mezcal production that help to define each. Firstly, mezcal can be made from the heart of any agave plant and this is roasted rather than baked, giving mezcal its distinctive burnt, smoky flavours. Mezcal can also be distilled just once, however, it is usually distilled twice for the international market and must be bottled if exported. The biggest misconception of tequila is that it contains a worm (moth larva) but this is actually mezcal, not tequila.

CATEGORIES AND STYLES

Tequila is categorised according to both the percentage of agave spirit it contains and the period of maturation it undergoes.

Mixto: contains at least 51% blue agave distillate, the rest being made up of industrial spirit or spirit made from molasses, brown sugar or any other sugar type.

Pura: 100% agave distillate.

White (blanco/plata/silver/platino): clear/white tequila, which has been aged for a maximum of 60 days.

Gold (oro): made in the same way as white but with the addition of flavouring and colouring, usually caramel.

Reposado (rested): means rested in Spanish. Must be aged in oak for a minimum of 60 days and a maximum of one year.

Aged (añejo): Mexican law states that for a tequila to be given the title of aged it must be sealed in government oak barrels for over one year which must be no larger than 600 litres.

CURADOS

Curados are flavoured tequilas. Common flavours include lemon, orange, strawberry and pineapple. These can be used for flavouring cocktails and also served straight.

Brands

Each distillery will have its own unique brands that are bottled at varying ages. Here are some of the more popular international brands although there are hundreds available in Mexico.

Agavero tequila liqueur (32% ABV)

Arette
Arette Añejo (38% ABV)
Arette Blanco (38% ABV)
Arette Grin Clase (38% ABV)
Arette Unique (38% ABV)

Corralejo
Corralejo Añejo (38% ABV)
Corralejo Reposado (38% ABV)

Don Julio
Don Julio Añejo (38% ABV)
Don Julio Blanco (38% ABV)
Don Julio Reposado (38% ABV)

Gran Centenario
Gran Centenario Añejo (38% ABV)
Gran Centenario Plata (38% ABV)
Gran Centenario Reposado
  (38% ABV)

Herradura
Herradura Añejo (40% ABV)
Herradura Blanco (40% ABV)
Herradura Reposado (40% ABV)

Jose Cuervo
Jose Cuervo Classico (38% ABV)
Jose Cuervo Gold (38% ABV)
Jose Cuervo Reposado (38% ABV)
Jose Cuervo Reserva de Familia
  (40% ABV)
Sierra Añejo (40% ABV)
Sierra Reposado (38% ABV)
Sierra Silver (38% ABV)
1800 Coleccion (38% ABV)

Maracame
Maracame Añejo (40% ABV)
Maracame Platino (40% ABV)
Maracame Reposado (40% ABV)

Olmeca Tequila
Olmeca Gold (40% ABV)
Olmeca Silver (40% ABV)

Partida Tequila
Partida Añejo (40% ABV)
Partida Blanco (40% ABV)
Partida Reposado (40% ABV)

Patron
Gran Patron Platinum (40% ABV)
Patron XO Café (35% ABV)

Porfidio
Porfidio Añejo (38% ABV)
Porfidio Plata (38% ABV)

Sauza
Sauza Añejo – Conmemorativo
  (40% ABV)
Sauza Blanco (38% ABV)
Sauza Extra Gold (38% ABV)
Sauza Hornitos (38% ABV)

Mezcal brands
Hacienda de Chihuahua (38% ABV)
Hacienda de Chihuahua Sotol (38% ABV)
Lajita (40% ABV)
Monte Alban (40% ABV)

ESSENTIAL SERVES

Tequila has a certain reputation as a drink that should be served with salt and lemon and knocked back in one. This is still largely the case, although tequila has fast become a trendy category and offers a myriad of choice in how it is served, in long drinks and with cocktails.

Tequila and tonic is a surprisingly refreshing alternative to the popular G&T. Orange and cola are also served with tequila as a long drink. The most famous cocktail to include tequila is the Margarita, using Cointreau and fresh lime, and serving it straight up or on the rocks with a salt rim.

As with rums, aged tequilas can have the sipping qualities of some fine cognacs or whiskies. Try an Añejo Old Fashioned for good measure.

DISTILLED KNOWLEDGE ABOUT TEQUILA
- Tequila is a plant distillate, which must be made from at least 51% blue agave.
- The blue agave looks like a cactus but in fact it is part of the lily family and takes between eight to 10 years to fully mature.
- It can only be made in the specified five states in Mexico, surrounding the town of Tequila, in the state of Jalisco.
- Tequila must be bottled between 35–55% ABV but most tequilas are bottled at 38 or 40% ABV.

FRUIT DISTILLATES:

Most fruits can be used as the base for making a distillate, however the most popular choice is grapes, which are used to make brandy. Other fruits that are popularly used in the production of spirits are apples, pears and plums.

BRANDY

Although the history of brandy is vague, by the late 13th century, brandy or aqua vitae (literally 'water of life'), was being consumed with great pleasure by Popes and Holy Roman Emperors who described it as geprant Wein, or 'burnt wine', which was changed into brandewijn by the Dutch and then 'brandy' by the English.

PRODUCTION

Brandy, or eau de vie, is referred to as a fruit distillate and is made by distilling fermented fruit juices. The majority of the world's brandies are made by using fermented grape juice (e.g. wine), the most famous being the French brandies of Cognac and Armagnac.

Brandies are made around the world, mainly in wine-producing countries, including Chile, England, Germany, Greece, Italy, Mexico, Peru, Portugal, South Africa, Spain and the USA. Other popular fruits used to make brandy include apples, pears, plums and cherries.

The majority of non-grape brandies (also labelled eau de vie) are produced by using column distillation and are often reduced then bottled straight from the still, and are generally clear in colour. These tend to be fruit brandies, such as plum brandy (Slivovitz) and grappa (Italian eau de vie). Often liqueurs are labelled as a brandy, for example cherry brandy, however, they are not technically a brandy as they are produced by steeping fruit in a grape spirit and not by distilling the fermented juices of the fruit.

Brandy made from grapes, however, generally uses pot distillation (known in France as alembiques) and matures in wood, giving brandy its signature golden colour and unique flavours.

COGNAC

The most famous of brandies is cognac. Cognac is a fine French brandy (a blend of eaux de vie) from the region around the town of Cognac in western France. The region is recognised with its own appellation contrôlée and in order for it to be labelled so, it must be made from grapes grown in the Charente and Charente-Maritime departments, which are divided into six sub-regions reflecting variations in climate and soil.

These regions produce three kinds of grape: Ugni Blanc, Folle Blanche and Colombard, however, 90% of the wine produced for cognac is from the Ugni Blanc grape. These are harvested, crushed and the juice extracted for fermentation, which produces a wine of about 8–9% ABV.

By law, cognac must be double-distilled in copper pot stills, using the traditional Charentais stills, to produce a spirit with a maximum 72% ABV; this is referred to as eau de vie. Distillation must be completed by 31st March following the harvest as the change in climate can start a second fermentation.

This eau de vie must then be matured in French oak casks, usually from the forests of Limoges. The casks are usually 350 litres, to allow a high ratio of the cognac to be in contact with the wood. Unlike other spirits, cognac is then blended by transferring the ageing spirits from barrel to barrel. To be labelled cognac it must contain a minimum of two different eaux de vie; some can contain over 100 different eaux de vie. Under the legislation of the appellation contrôlée, caramel, sugar syrup and boise (wood chippings) can be added to the barrels to speed up the rate of ageing, however the best cognacs simply let the wood and blending do the talking. The cognacs are then placed in large glass vessels and allowed to marry. The spirit is then reduced to a minimum strength of 40% ABV, and usually to a maximum of 50%, with distilled or demineralised water.

COGNAC BRANDS

Brands generally fall into three classifications and price ranges: VSs tend to be house-pouring brands, VSOPs tend to be premium pouring brands and XOs are the super premium expensive brands.

Courvoisier, Hennessey, Martell and Remy Martin account for around 80% of all cognac sold outside of France. Below is some information on the main brands that produce a range of cognacs.

Bisquit
Bisquit VSOP (40% ABV)
Bisquit XO (40% ABV)

Camus
Camus Borderies XO (40% ABV)
Camus Extra (40% ABV)
Camus Grand VSOP (40% ABV)
Camus Josephine (40% ABV)

Courvoisier
Courvoisier Napoleon (40% ABV)
Courvoisier VS (40% ABV)
Courvoisier VS Exclusif (40% ABV)
Courvoisier VSOP (40% ABV)
Courvoisier XO (40% ABV)
L'Esprit de Courvoisier (40% ABV)

Delamain Pale and Dry (40% ABV)

Frapin
Frapin Château de Fontpinot (40% ABV)
Frapin VIP XO (40% ABV)
Frapin VSOP (40% ABV)

Hennessey
Hennessey Fine de Cognac (40% ABV)
Hennessey Paradis (40% ABV)
Hennessey Privilege VSOP (40% ABV)
Hennessey Pure White (40% ABV)
Hennessey Ricard (40% ABV)
Hennessey VS (40% ABV)
Hennessey XO (40% ABV)

Hine
Hine Antique Très Rare (40% ABV)
Hine Family Reserve (40% ABV)
Hine Rare and Delicate (40% ABV)
Hine Signature (40% ABV)

Martell
Martell Cordon Bleu (40% ABV)
Reserve De Martell (40% ABV)
Martell VSOP (40% ABV)

Ragnaud-Sabourin
Ragnaud-Sabourin No. 10 (40% ABV)
Ragnaud-Sabourin No. 35 (43% ABV)
Ragnaud-Sabourin Paradis (43% ABV)

Remy Martin
Remy Martin Extra (40% ABV)
Remy Martin Louis XIII (40% ABV)
Remy Martin VS Grand Cru (40% ABV)
Remy Martin VSOP (40% ABV)
Remy Martin XO Special (40% ABV)

COGNAC TERMS

VS – Very Special or 3 Star: budget cognac, the youngest eau de vie in the blend, must be at least two years old.

VSOP – Very Special Old Pale or Reserve: must be aged for a minimum of four years.

XO – Extra Old or hors d'âge: must be aged for a minimum of six years, and is generally aged for at least 10 to 20 years.

Fine Grande Champagne: must be made from 100% Grande Champagne grape.

Fine Champagne: must be made from a minimum of 50% Grande Champagne grape with the remainder being from Petite Champagne grape.

ESSENTIAL SERVES

Young cognac (VS cognac) is generally served in long drinks, using carbonated mixers such as cola, lemonade and ginger ale. It is also more popularly used as a base in most of the classic cocktail categories, including the Brandy Buck, Brandy (Pierre) Collins, Brandy Sour, Brandy Flip, Brandy Crusta, Brandy Julep, Brandy Sling and the most famous of all, the Brandy Alexander.

The more mature cognacs are again best left for more sophisticated uses, such as sipping after dinner from a large brandy balloon, accompanied by a cigar, or being used as the base for a classic twist, such as the Brandy Old Fashioned.

DISTILLED KNOWLEDGE ABOUT COGNAC
- The main grape varieties used in French brandy production are Ugni Blanc, Folle Blanche and Colombard.
- It takes around 10 litres of wine to produce 1 litre of eau de vie.
- Distillation must be completed by March 31st following the harvest.
- The minimum ageing for marketable cognac is 24 months following the end of the distillation period.
- Phylloxera vastatrix louse (yellow lethal vine pest) almost destroyed brandy production in the 1860s.
- Unaged brandy is called eau de vie (or aqua vitae).

ARMAGNAC

Armagnac comes from the region of Gascony in the south west of France and was produced before cognac. Armagnac producers use the same main grapes as cognac, but the primary difference is the use of the hybrid of the Folle Blanche and Noah grape varieties. However, the use of this hybrid will be phased out by 2010 in accordance with French law. Armagnac is made in a similar way to cognac, but Armagnac is only usually distilled once to between 53–70% and is aged in black oak. Unlike cognac, Armagnac produces vintages, with some years better than others.

There are three regions in Armagnac:
Bas produces the best and most wines used in Armagnac and produces flavours of plums and prunes from its sandy soil.

Ténarèze produces around 40% of wine used in Armagnac, which give floral notes, particularly violets, from its clay soil.

Haut Armagnac only produces a small amount of wine, with chalky soil and a chalky flavour.

Armagnac terms
Armagnac: 2–6 years old
Vieil Armagnac: over 6 years old
Millesimes: must be over 10 years old

BRANDS

Baron de Sigognac VS (40% ABV)
Baron de Sigognac 10 Year Old (40% ABV)
Baron de Sigognac VSOP (40% ABV)
Comte de Lauvia VSOP superior (40% ABV)
Comte de Lauvia VSOP superior 8 Year Old (40% ABV)
Comte de Lauvia XO imperial 12 Year Old (40% ABV)
Comte de Lauvia 15 Year Old (40% ABV)
Janneau Très Vieille Réserve (40% ABV)
Janneau VS (40% ABV)
Janneau VSOP (40% ABV)
Janneau 5 Year Old (40% ABV)
Janneau XO (40% ABV)
Marquis de Montesquiou Napoleon (40% ABV)
Marquis de Montesquiou 21 Year Old hors d'age (40% ABV)
Marquis de Montesquiou Imperial XO (40% ABV)

ESSENTIAL SERVES

Young Armagnac is generally served in a long drink, using carbonated mixers such as cola, lemonade and ginger ale. The more mature or vintage Armagnacs are best left for sipping after dinner.

DISTILLED KNOWLEDGE ABOUT ARMAGNAC
- Armagnac is the oldest French grape brandy, dating back to 1419.
- Armagnac is only usually distilled once to between 53–70% and is aged in black oak.
- Armagnac is often released in vintages.

AROMATISED/FORTIFIED WINES

Vermouth is classified as aromatised wine, and is based on wines that have been fortified with grape spirit and flavoured with herbs and spices. The word 'vermouth' comes from the German 'Vermud', meaning wormwood, a bitter aromatic plant.

Aromatised wines are made by infusing a base alcohol, usually grape spirit, with sugar, botanicals, caramel and water, and will be bottled to around 15–18%.

VERMOUTH TERMS

Dry (or extra dry): is the very pale amber coloured vermouth, which is crisp and like a dry white wine.
Sweet (rosso): is a red/burgundy coloured vermouth with a dry bitterness.
Bianco (medium): a herbal medium-sweet vermouth, usually light amber.

Rosé: this is the light pink colour vermouth that is slightly sweet and bitter.

Brands

Cinzano Bianco (15% ABV) – medium sweet white vermouth
Cinzano Extra Dry (15% ABV) – flavoured with 14 ingredients, including camomile and rose petals.
Cinzano Rosso (15% ABV) – sweet red vermouth flavoured with 35 ingredients.
Cynar (16.5% ABV) – an artichoke-based aperitif, dry and bitter.
Dubonnet Red (14.8% ABV) – five grape varietals with an infusion of herbs and spices.
Martini Bianco (14.7% ABV) – filtered through charcoal, flavoured with natural herbs and spices.
Martini Extra Dry (14.7% ABV) – dry wine vermouth.
Martini Rosso (18% ABV) – addition of caramel and contains 155–60 g sugar per litre.
Noilly Prat (18% ABV) – dry and sweet versions aged in Canadian oak and blended with 20 herbs and spices.
Punt E Mes (16% ABV) – orange bitter-sweet aperitif with quinine.
Vya Extra Dry (16% ABV) – white wine, herbal, floral and spicy.
Vya Sweet (16% ABV) – orange muscat wine with dried citrus notes.

ESSENTIAL SERVES

Vermouths and aromatised wines can be served as an aperitif neat or on the rocks and with a twist of citrus peel (lemon or orange). More commonly though they are served as tall drinks with a carbonated mixer such as soda, lemonade or ginger ale and in classic cocktails including the Americano, Negroni, Manhattan and Dry Martini.

OTHER FORTIFIED WINES

Other popular fortified wines include sherry, port and Madeira.

Sherry
Generally made sweet and dry and in Spain. Styles of sherry include Fino ('fine'), Manzanilla, Amontillado, Oloroso ('scented'), Palo Cortado, Moscatel and Pedro Ximenez.

Port
Made in Portugal and aged in wooden barrels, it is generally much thicker, richer and sweeter than sherry but contains a higher alcohol content than most other wines.

Madeira
Madeira is made on the island of the same name. The wine is baked in ovens and aged for a minimum of eight years to give its unique flavour.

BITTERS

Originally made by monks and apothecaries, bitters are the origins of medicinal spirits used in drinks. Bitters are made by blending botanicals in spirit, which is then often aged in oak. Most producers' recipes are a closely guarded secret and contain over 30 different herbs, roots, berries, flowers and fruits that are macerated or infused with the raw spirit.

There are two main styles of bitters: bar bitters that are used in very small amounts to add a dry, smooth edge to certain cocktails, and pouring bitters that are mostly drunk as an aperitif or digestif, due to the digestive properties of the ingredients.

BAR BITTERS

There are two types of bar bitters: aromatic and fruit/spiced. Bartenders the world over have begun to formulate their very own styles of bitter.

Aromatic bitters

Angostura is the most famous of the bitters developed around 1830 by Dr Siegert, a German surgeon in Simon Bolivar's army in Venezuela. These dark bitters are bottled at 44.7% ABV and have a distinctive clove and anise flavour and aroma. Another well known brand of bitters is Peychaud's. These purple bitters were developed by Antoine Peychaud in the early 1800s in New Orleans.

Fruit and spiced bitters

These come in the form of orange, grapefruit, pineapple. Recent additions include cardamom, vanilla, cinnamon, clove and many other types of fruit and spiced bitters.

POURING BITTERS

Pouring bitters generally come in much larger bottles, ranging from 500 ml to 1 litre and are bottled in the same way as spirits and liqueurs. Be sure to use small quantities of these in mixed drinks as they will overpower a drink if used liberally.

Amer Picon (21% ABV) is a French dry sweet bitters.

Aperol (11% ABV) is an orange, quinine-flavoured pouring bitters from Italy.

Campari is an Italian blend of botanicals, neutral alcohol, sugar and purified water. Usually bottled between 20–28% ABV.

Fernet Branca (40% ABV) is an Italian digestif bitters with a mint version called Branca Menta.

Jägermeister (35% ABV) is a German bitters containing over 50 botanicals and is generally served chilled from the fridge or freezer.

Underberg (44% ABV) is a digestif bitters from Germany.

Unicum (40% ABV) is a Hungarian herbal bitter liqueur drunk as both and aperitif and a digestif.

LIQUEURS

It is believed monks were amongst the first to discover liqueurs, experimenting with the medicinal properties of herbs, flowers and spices with alcohols. Benedictine, developed in the early 16th century and believed to be the first liqueur ever made, is still around today.

PRODUCTION

Liqueurs are made by flavouring or re-distilling spirits with fruits, nuts, cream, herbs, spices, flowers, roots, plants and other botanicals. There are several ways of producing liqueurs and the majority of liqueurs will use one or a combination of the following production methods:

Maceration: the fruit and botanicals are steeped in cold alcohol.
Infusion: the fruit and botanicals are steeped in warm alcohol (usually 40–50ºC/104–122ºF).
Percolation: this is a more intensive method of maceration, whereby pure alcohol is passed through the fruit and botanicals to extract the flavour.
Distillation: the fruit and botanicals are distilled with the neutral alcohol to produce a clear distillate.

Maturation: some liqueurs are matured in oak to pick up more complex flavours and to 'marry' before being reduced with water to bottling strength.

According to European guidelines a liqueur must be bottled to a minimum of 15% ABV and usually to around 30% ABV, and have a content of at least 100 g of sugar per litre, although this is often much higher. Liqueurs bottled at around 23% ABV are known as 'demi-fines' and will contain a sugar content of approximately 200–250 g per litre. Liqueurs bottled at around 28–30% ABV are known as 'fines' and contain 400–450 g of sugar per litre. 'Surfines' will have a minimum alcoholic strength of 30% ABV and a sugar content of 450–500 g per litre.

The ingredients that are marked with this symbol ▲, indicate those liqueurs that ignite without too much persuasion (which are often used in pousse-cafés and cocktails). Please take extreme precaution when dealing with fire.

TYPES AND BRANDS OF LIQUEURS

Liqueurs can be classified into various categories, which include cream, nut, fruit, herb and spice liqueurs, although some liqueurs can encompass more than one category. Here are some of the most popular brands and flavours that a professional bartender should know.

Cream liqueurs
Advocaat (20% ABV): a Dutch liqueur made with egg yolk and brandy, and flavoured with vanilla, lemon, cherry and oranges.
Amarula (17% ABV): flavoured from the fruit of the Marula tree, also known as the elephant tree, with a rich, creamy vanilla and chocolate fruitiness.
Baileys Irish Cream (17% ABV): sweet whiskey-flavoured cream liqueur.
Castries Cream (16% ABV): St Lucian nut cream liqueur.
Mozart (34% ABV): chocolate liqueurs available in white, dark and milk chocolate and made in Austria.

Nut liqueurs

Amaretto (26–28% ABV): rich brown Italian brandy-based liqueur made from almond extract, apricot stones and seeds, and sweetened with sugar. There are a number of amarettos, the most famous being Di Saronno Amaretto Originale.

Frangelico (24% ABV): Italian wild hazelnut liqueur, brown in colour.

Fruit liqueurs

Alize (16% ABV): yellow and red coloured liqueurs flavoured with passion fruit and cranberry.

Apricot brandy (30% ABV): apricot liqueur with a brandy base.

Archers Peach Schnapps (23% ABV): clear, peach flavoured schnapps.

Cherry brandy (30% ABV): cherry flavoured liqueur with a brandy base.

Cherry Heering (24.7% ABV): cherry flavoured liqueur with the characteristic hint of almond and a secret mix of herbs and spices.

Chambord (17% ABV): black raspberry and honey liqueur from Burgundy, France.

Clement Shrubb (40% ABV): orange flavoured rum-based liqueur.

Cointreau ▲ (40% ABV): a sweet, colourless liqueur, orange in flavour, and made in France.

Crème de … (17–30% ABV): this French term usually denotes a liqueur of a rather thick consistency and the crème de … will be followed by the French term for the fruit, for instance Crème de framboise or Crème de banane. Other types of liqueur flavours include: cassis (blackcurrant), fraise (strawberry), framboise (raspberry), mure (blackberry), pêche (peach), menthe (mint), noix (nut), banane (banana), cacao (cocoa), myrtilles (blueberries), poire William (Williams pear), maraschino (cherry), abricot (apricot).

Cuarenta Y Tres (31% ABV): translates as forty-three in Spanish. A vanilla flavoured liqueur from Spain made from 43 different herbs and spices.

Curaçao (15–23% ABV): made from the dried peel from the bitter Larahas curaçao orange and named after the island of Curaçao. It comes in various colours, including orange, blue, green and red.

Grand Marnier ▲ (40% ABV): French cognac flavoured with orange. Light yellow in colour.

Kwai Feh (20% ABV): lychee liqueur.

Limoncello (25–30% ABV): Italian lemon flavoured liqueur.

Malibu (21% ABV): a clear brand of coconut rum.

Mandarine Napoleon ▲ (38% ABV): tangerine flavoured liqueur.

Maraschino (20–32% ABV): sour cherry liqueur with a dry edge.

Midori (20% ABV): a green, melon flavoured liqueur.

Passoã (20% ABV): passion fruit liqueur.

Pimms No.1 (25% ABV): red, herbal, bittersweet gin-based liqueur.

Pisang Ambon (21% ABV): banana, fruit and herb flavoured liqueur.

Sloe gin (15–30% ABV): gin-based liqueur made with sloe berries.

Southern Comfort (40% ABV): liqueur with a bourbon base and peach flavouring.

Herb and spice liqueurs

Absinthe ▲ (68–80% ABV): also known as the Green Fairy and not strictly a liqueur, absinthe takes its name from Artemisia absinthium, the botanical name for the bitter herb wormwood, known in French as 'grande absinthe'. Absinthe also contains the molecule thujone, which supposedly accounts for its alleged mind-altering properties.

Aftershock (40% ABV): available in red, blue and green, these liqueurs are cinnamon (red), citrus (blue) and aniseed (green) flavoured.

Agavero (32% ABV): a tequila liqueur made from 100% agave, generally has a floral vanilla taste.

Benedictine ▲ (40% ABV): a sweet, golden, brandy-based liqueur originally produced by monks in Normandy, France.

Chartreuse ▲ (40–55% ABV): French liqueur flavoured with many herbs and spices, available in yellow (40% ABV) and green (55% ABV).

Crème de menthe (25% ABV): white or green liqueur distilled from a concentrate of mint leaves.

Drambuie ▲ (40% ABV): Scotch whisky liqueur, flavoured with heather honey and herbs, light yellow in colour.

Galliano ▲ (30% ABV): a golden coloured Italian liqueur, flavoured with liquorice and aniseed.

Glayva (35% ABV): Scottish whisky liqueur with orange, honey and herb flavours.

Hierbas (22–40% ABV): Spanish honey and herb flavoured liqueur with hints of aniseed.

Illy Coffee Liqueur (30% ABV): coffee flavoured Italian liqueur.

Kahlúa (26.5% ABV): cane spirit flavoured with arabica coffee beans.

Krupnik (40% ABV): Polish honey and spice liqueur with a vodka base.

Opal Nera (40% ABV): a rich purple black aniseed liqueur made in Italy.

Ouzo ▲ (38–40% ABV): a Greek liqueur made from grapes and flavoured with spices, including anise, coriander and cinnamon.

Pastis ▲ (40–45% ABV): anise and liquorice liqueur.

Patron XO (35% ABV): tequila-based coffee liqueur.

Pernod ▲ (40–45% ABV): French anise and liquorice liqueur.

Ron Miel Canario (30% ABV): honey flavoured rum from the Canary Islands.

Sambuca ▲ (40% ABV): Italian aniseed flavoured liqueur.

Strega (40% ABV): an Italian liqueur made from over 70 different herbs and spices.

Tia Maria (26.5% ABV): a brown coffee flavoured liqueur.

Toussaint liqueur (26.5% ABV): – a Haitian coffee flavoured liqueur.

Tuaca (35% ABV): Italian vanilla and orange flavoured liqueur with a brandy base.

Xante (38% ABV): a pear flavoured liqueur with a cognac base.

Serving absinthe Czech-style

1) Pour a shot of absinthe into a glass over a teaspoon of sugar so that it absorbs the absinthe.

2) Light the sugar and let it burn so that it bubbles and caramelises.

3) Pour the melted sugar into the absinthe and stir (if the glass catches alight, quickly smother the flames).

4) Add 1 to 2 parts water to the absinthe and serve.

Serving absinthe French-style

1) Pour one shot of absinthe into a glass.

2) Place a slatted absinthe spoon on the glass and place one or two sugar lumps on the spoon.

3) Slowly our 4 to 6 parts iced water through the sugar and into the absinthe.

4) Stir the mixture which will turn cloudy, and serve.

WINE AND CHAMPAGNE

Wine and champagne are an exciting and vast area of product knowledge, and all bartenders should know their Pinot Grigio from their Sauvignon Blanc. This section will endeavour to lay the foundations of knowledge and practical application of wine and champagne service.

STYLES OF WINE

There are five widely accepted broad categories wine falls into, these being white, red, rosé, sparkling and dessert wines. The names of different wine styles derive, generally, from the grapes used to make that wine. Some are blends while others are of one variety. Grapes are the main source of wine, although wine can be made from almost any fruit.

The grape variety is of great importance in shaping a wine style. In basic terms, red grapes will produce red wine (although you can get white wine from red grapes) and white grapes will produce white wine. The choice of grape will also influence such factors as the acidity level, alcohol, tannin levels and the body and style of the wine. There are literally dozens of white and red grape varietals around the world that will produce a certain style of wine and they are often made as a single varietal wine (such as Chenin Blanc) and less commonly as a blend (Châteauneuf-du-Pape, which has no less than 13 varietals).

White

Popular white wines can broadly be arranged into several varietals which include Chardonnay, Chenin Blanc, Semillon, Riesling and Sauvignon Blanc.

Light: Sauvignon Blanc
Medium: Riesling, Chardonnay, Chenin Blanc
Heavy: Semillon

Red

Popular red wines can also be categorised into the main varietals which include Merlot, Shiraz, Grenache, Pinot Noir and Cabernet Sauvignon. Other popular international red varietals worth noting are Pinotage from South Africa and Tempranillo from Spain.

Light: Pinot Noir
Medium: Merlot, Grenache, Cabernet Sauvignon
Heavy: Shiraz

Rosé

France and Spain are the main producers of this style, however, countries around the world are producing some great examples. Predominantly a mix of red and white grape varieties – more white than red – and now enjoying a bit of a comeback.

Light: Rosé de Loire, Rosé d'Anjou and some white Zinfandels
Medium: Rosado, Grenache
Heavy: white Zinfandel and some Grenache

Sparkling

Sparkling wine is made throughout the world, with many countries registering names for their own unique style, most famously Champagne or Prosecco. Sparkling wine is usually white or rosé but there are examples of red Australian sparkling Shiraz.

Cava from Spain
Prosecco from Italy
Champagne is from the Champagne region of France only

Dessert

Also known as pudding wines, these are sweet and are served chilled after dinner in small glasses due to their higher strength. Popular wines include Sauternes and Tokaji Aszu.

OPENING A BOTTLE OF CHAMPAGNE

Place the bottle on a flat surface, remove the foil top and start to loosen the wire cage.

Wrap one hand around the cork (keeping your thumb firmly on the cork) and with the other grip the bottle and turn it.

Continue to turn the bottle until the cork comes free and you hear a gentle pop. Don't be tempted to pull out the cork.

SERVING TEMPERATURES		
Wine type	°C	°F
Sparkling wine	6–12	42–54
Rosé wine	9–12	48–54
White wine	9–14	48–58
Sherry (light)	9–14	48–58
Red wine	13–20	57–68
Fortified wine	13–20	57–68
Sherry (dark)	13–20	57–68

WINE GLASSES

All glasses should be spotlessly clean and checked thoroughly for finger marks as well as any other unsightly marks. Wine glasses are very delicate so gently dry them down with a clean, soft glass towel. The shape of a wine glass can impact on the taste of the wine, and for this reason different types of wine are served in different glasses. The four main types of wine glasses are:

White wine glasses: tulip shaped
Red wine glasses: more rounded and have a larger bowl
Sparkling wine flutes: tall and thin
Dessert wine glasses: short and thin

A suitable all-purpose wine glass should hold 10 oz of liquid, be transparent to allow the taster to examine the colour of the wine and its body, and have a slight curve inwards at the top to hold in the bouquet. While an all-purpose wine glass is fine for serving a red wine, do not serve a white wine in a red wine glass – this is not the done thing!

WINE SERVING TEMPERATURES

Just as important as wine glasses is the temperature at which wines are served, as temperature has a huge impact on taste. Serving wine cool will mask some imperfections – good for young or cheap wines – while a warmer wine temperature allows expression of the wine's characteristics – ideal with older or more expensive wines. The chart above shows the serving temperatures of different wines.

A bottle of wine will cool 2°C (36°F) for every ten minutes in the refrigerator, and will warm at about this same rate when removed from the refrigerator and left at room temperature – the temperature of the room will affect the speed with which the wine warms up, so if you are bartending in the Caribbean some red wines are best served slightly cool. If you need to chill a bottle of wine in a hurry, twenty minutes in the freezer will do the trick.

Note: never put Champagne in the freezer... ever!

PRESENTING AND OPENING WINE AT A TABLE

When presenting wine, ensure the person who ordered the wine is presented the wine with the label facing them, this should be brief and fuss-free. Opening wine should never be rushed. Use a flat surface on a free table close by or if there is room use the guests' table. Rest the bottle on the table and ensure the cork exits gently, with no popping – this is good etiquette.

Present the wine, label facing the guest.

Cut the foil neatly from the top off the bottle.

Using a cork screw, pierce the cork in the centre and twist gently.

Use the metal arm to brace against the lip of the bottle.

Gently release the cork.

Pouring wine at a table

Once open, always pour a small amount into the host's glass for sampling. If accepted fill the glasses no more than two-thirds (about 5–6 oz) – a glass can always be refilled – then pour the same quantity into the remaining guests' glasses, preferably starting with the eldest lady to the youngest, then

eldest gentleman to the youngest (if the set-up isn't conducive to this, then just go round the table and make sure everyone is served). Not overfilling the glass will allow your guests to swirl the wine, smell the bouquet and check out the wine's 'legs'. Still wines should be poured towards the centre of the glass, while sparkling wines should be poured against the side to preserve bubbles. To control drips, twist the bottle slightly as you tilt it upright.

WINE CHECKLIST

- Serving wine correctly can add finesse and style to your bar operation.
- All glasses should be spotlessly clean.
- Wine temperature is very important (refer to chart on page 89 for details).
- For table service, present the wine to the host and ensure the label is on display.
- Never shake a bottle of wine.
- Open with confidence and never pop open a bottle; ease the cork out gently.
- Always pour to the host/person who orders the wine first, then fill the glass no more than two-thirds.
- Place white wine bottles into a wine bucket and dress the bottle with a wine towel; leave red wine bottles on the table.

MYTHS ABOUT WINE

- It is a popular fallacy that a wine is said to be corked when the bottle opener has gone through the other end of the cork and pieces of cork are pushed into the wine, or that the cork has crumbled into the wine over time, affecting the taste. This couldn't be further from the truth. Bear in mind though, that you should never pierce the cork all the way through, as small pieces of cork will fall into the wine.

- Crumbling corks simply mean poor quality cork, not bad wine! If you do find pieces of cork in the wine, sieve it into a decanter. Corked wine occurs when the cork is tainted with a chemical called TCA (trichloroanisole), leaving a musty and damp smell and taste in the drink. It is estimated that nearly 5% of the world's wines are corked. Note that many wine producers are now opting for plastic corks, which never produce corked wine.

- Another common misconception is that red wines should be served warm. This is not the case. The ideal serving temperature for many fine red wines is between 14–18°C (57–64°F), so the term room temperature really isn't accurate enough. Many reds, unless stored somewhere cool, will benefit from half an hour in the refrigerator. This is particularly the case for Beaujolais and young Burgundy, as well as Pinot Noir from the New World. Good clarets, Rhônes and other reds from warmer climates are generally fine served at between 16–18°C (61–64°F).

BEERS

The production methods and styles of beer vary across the world. This chapter gives a consolidated insight into the world of beers.

ORIGINS

Beer has been consumed for thousands of years, as far back as the Egyptians, circa 2400 BC, and is considered to be one of the world's oldest alcoholic beverages. The earliest known chemical evidence of beer dates to circa 3500–3100 BC. It is likely that is was independently invented among various cultures throughout the world as almost any substance containing carbohydrates, namely sugar or starch, can naturally undergo fermentation.

PRODUCTION

In basic terms beer is made from malted grains, hops and water, and allowed to ferment with the addition of yeast. The liquid is then strained and transferred to tanks allowing it to mellow. It is then carbonated and packed accordingly.

STYLES OF BEER

Originating in mainland Europe, the styles of beer are vast and varied and are today made around the world.

Pilsner: a light, dry lager, originally made in the town of Pilsen in the Czech Republic and uses Saaz hops and bottom fermenting yeasts.

American light beer: mass produced in a similar way to Pilsner but generally much lighter in colour and flavour.

Malt liquors: these are usually of a higher alcohol percentage than regular beers (up to 14–16%) and are recognised as barley wine in the UK.

STYLES OF ALE

Ales are defined by the strain of yeast used and the fermenting temperature. They are normally brewed with top-fermenting yeasts (known as Saccharomyces cerevisiae), and fermented between 15–24°C (59 and 75°F).

Bitter (AKA amber ale): traditionally from the United Kingdom it can range from a light amber to a deep, dark colour and will generally have a slightly bitter taste.

Brown ale: a sweet dark ale, famed by Newcastle Brown ale.

Real ale: also known as cask-conditioned beer. The fundamental distinction between real and other ales is that the yeast is still present in the container from which the beer is served, although it will have settled to the bottom and is not poured into the glass. Because the yeast is still alive, the process of fermentation continues in the cask or bottle on the way to the consumer, ensuring a fresh and natural taste.

Stout: high in hops and made using roasted barley, giving it its intensely dark colour. The most famous brand is Guinness, however, stout comes in three different styles including Irish, milk and imperial. Irish has a creamy head with a burnt flavour; milk stout is generally sweetened and imperial stout, originally made for Russian tsars, is much dryer and very strong.

Wheat beer: Pauliner and Hoegaarden are two popular wheat beers, unsurprisingly made from wheat and top fermented, and generally sweet and pale in colour. Also known as weiss, or white, beer.

SERVING AND POURING

Beers and ales are dispensed and packaged in various ways, using traditional kegs and draught dispensers, bottles and cans. The recommended temperature for serving beers or lagers is generally 6–9°C (43–48°F), and some are now super chilled to 1–3°C (34–37°F). Traditionally, ale is served at a higher temperature, around 10–13°C (50–55°F).

Pulling the perfect pint of lager

For a pint with minimal head it is a simple matter of holding the glass at a 45 degree angle close to the spout, and opening the tap. It's important to fully open the tap, or it will splutter, and there will be too much foam. When the glass is around 75% full, tilt the glass vertically and fill to the brim. Flip the pump back just as the beer fills the glass. If a little head is desirable, there are two alternatives: allow some distance between the spout and the liquid when pouring; with some taps you can flip the tap forward when the beer is about 1 cm (½ in) from the top of the glass and then press a button, which forces out beer mixed with air, creating a head.

Bitter on tap (e.g. John Smiths)

This should be poured in a similar manner to lager, but the characteristics of the beer generally lead to head being formed more easily. Some like more head than others and creating the right amount takes some practice!

Pulling the perfect pint of ale

Real ale, or pumped bitter (e.g. Abbot Ale) uses a rather different technique to other draught beers as this is the only type of ale that is actually 'pulled' from a pump. Pull down the pump strongly and smoothly, whilst minimising the distance between the glass and the pump nozzle. After the first pull, ensure the nozzle is clear of the beer surface before returning the pump to an upright position, otherwise you

may suck up the beer you just pulled! Pull more beer using the same technique until the pint is full; it should only take three or four pulls to fill the glass. Do not stop pumping until the glass overflows, as the inevitable head will cloud your view of the liquid level. After pulling your pint, make sure that the pump is returned to an upright position. Always maintain and clean the draught properly.

Pulling the perfect pint of stout (Guinness)

Although Guinness.com suggests holding the glass at an angle, it is safe to simply leave the glass on the drip tray and open up the pump, leaving you to complete the order or serve other customers. When the glass is about two-thirds full, flip up the tap, and leave the pint to settle for a minute or so. During this time the liquid should lose its cloudy appearance and become black with a white foamy head. Carefully lift the glass up to the tap and fill it to the brim. Due to the thick head you should even be able to slightly overfill the glass. Place on the bar to settle to perfection.

BOTTLED BEERS AND PPSS

Bottled lagers and PPSs (Premium Packaged Spirits, or alcopops) should always be presented with the label facing the customer. Always ask the guest if they would like a glass, and if available supply a frozen or frosted glass. Place the glass next to the bottle and be sure to open all bottles in front of the guest.

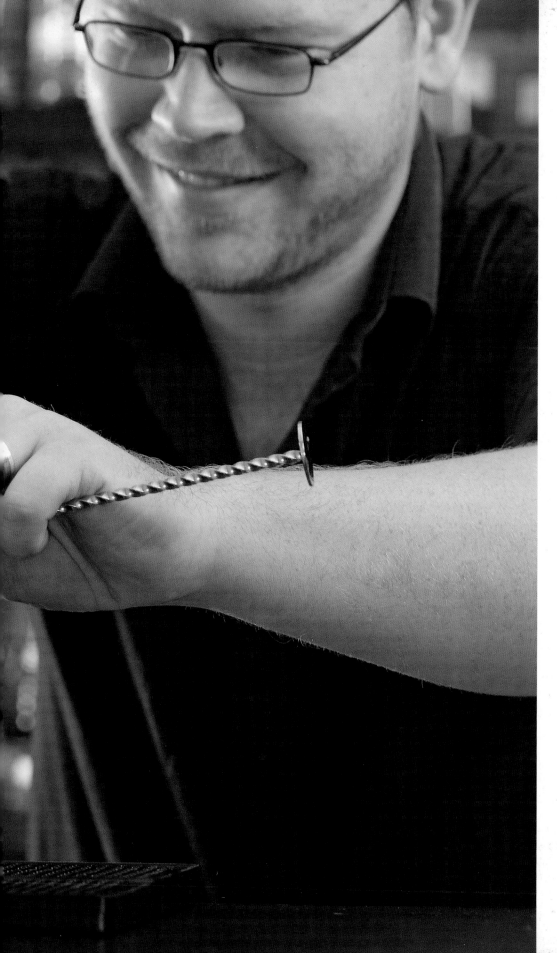

THE MECHANICS OF BARTENDING

THE MECHANICS OF BARTENDING

Bartenders should master the actions of preparing all types of drinks, as well as the techniques and processes involved.

THE ACTIONS OF A BARTENDER

The mechanics of bartending are a series of small and large, conscious and unconscious actions. Smiling, greeting, pouring, preparing, asking, shaking, muddling, icing, blending, cleaning, suggesting, clearing, wiping, rinsing, garnishing and stirring are just some of the mechanics of bartending.

This chapter aims to explain and illustrate the techniques and processes involved in bartending. Here is a step-by-step account of a customer transaction to demonstrate the no fewer than 40 different single actions involved in service, in this case a customer walks into a bar and orders a beer and a gin and tonic.

1) Bartender acknowledges the customer.
2) Wipes down the bar and places napkins in front of the customer.
3) Greets the customer and asks what they would like whilst clearing away an empty glass from the bar.
4) Customer orders a bottle of beer and a gin and tonic. Bartender rinses their hands under the tap and dries on apron.
5) Evaluates customer for age and intoxication.
6) Asks if they want a glass for the beer. Grabs glasses and suggests an upsell to the spirit. Asks the customer if they would like anything else.
7) Ices glass and places on the bar mat whilst adding up the total in their head.
8) Tells the customer up front what it would cost.
9) Fetches the premium gin. Presents the label for approval.
10) Acknowledges a new customer approaching.
11) Picks up mixer or gun with other hand and pours spirit and mixer into glass over ice. Returns mixer/gun and returns the bottle to the right place, label forward.
12) Makes a little bit of small talk whilst garnishing drink, using other hand to take a straw. Stirs drink with straw.
13) Opens fridge and fetches beer. Closes fridge. Opens beer and discards top in bin.
14) Presents drinks on napkins and repeats the cost to the customer.
15) Bartender calls out the note saying 'that's a ....' and takes the note.

16) Logs in to EPOS whilst calculating the right change in their head. Enters transaction in EPOS and checks the total. Picks up the change tray and returns the change and receipt on the change tray.
17) Thanks the customer and ensures the workspace was clear before proceeding to the next guest.

POURING

There are two ways of measuring spirits and juices, either by using a measured pour (using a jigger or thimble measure) or by free-pouring. There are a number of principles to remember when pouring:

- Always pour with the label facing the customer.
- If using a jigger pour directly over the glass to minimise spillage.
- Pour with the pour spout vertical to ensure a constant flow of liquid.
- Free-pouring should be practised and tested constantly, by using an Exacto Pour or a jigger.

- Be sure to pour accurately as this can affect the taste of the drink and profits.

The measured pour

Bartenders are not robots and will generally have their own exceptional style. It is important for each bartender to develop their own style and adapt that style to the environment they are working in.

Free-pouring

When practising new pouring techniques all you need is a bottle, pour spout, glass and lots of water. Practice makes perfect. Only when you have perfected the basic techniques of free-pouring should you practise accuracy. Here are some of the most popularly used free-pouring techniques.

Regular grip (twist/motorbike grip): this technique of free-pouring is the most commonly used in cocktail bars. It's fast, effective and stylish. Grasp the neck of the bottle firmly so that your knuckles are in line with the air hole on the pour spout.

Reverse grip: the exact opposite of a regular grip. This grip may be used to describe a grasp on any part of the bottle. This grip is utilised on both bottles and shaker tins.

Pop pour: using a regular grip pour the liquid into a glass. Once the measure is poured sharply force down the bottle towards the glass and then quickly upwards. This forces the liquid back up into the bottle, allowing the bottle to be dragged across to the next glass to pour, without spillage.

Reverse pop pour: the same method as the pop pour applies here but use a reverse grip instead of a regular grip.

Queen's grip: essentially a regular grip on the shoulder of the bottle, however, the fingers are spread further apart, reaching towards the bottom of the bottle. This grip is used primarily on unusually shaped or short bottles, such as Cointreau, Chambord or Drambuie bottles.

The measured pour

Regular grip

Reverse grip

Pop pour

Reverse pop

Queen's grip

COCKTAIL METHODOLOGY

All cocktails require a method of preparation. As with cookery, you will need to know the methodology before you start combining flavours. Understanding how and why a method is used for a particular drink forms the fundamental foundations of the modern mixologist, and all who grace the stage of a cocktail bar should know the basics of building, stirring, muddling, shaking, straining and the various other methods of preparing proper drinks.

COCKTAIL PREPARATION METHODS

The techniques of proper drink making are the fundamentals of bartending and the methodology of preparing drinks impacts on the final product dramatically. Let's take, as an example, the ingredients of the Daiquiri and the Caipirissima, both of which use the same three ingredients: rum, lime and sugar. The ingredients may be the same, but two entirely different results will be produced depending on whether the ingredients are shaken or muddled. Muddling will produce a Caipirissima, shaking a Daiquiri. The main techniques of drink preparation are as follows:

Build

This is the most basic method of preparing drinks. Simply add the ingredients (usually by adding the cheapest ingredients first, or in order of the recipe) to an ice-filled glass, stir thoroughly, then garnish and add a straw (where appropriate).

Accuracy

In order to free-pour accurately, bartenders should use their internal body clock to count the measure of liquid being poured. The most common way of measuring free-pouring accurately is to use the bubble method: as soon as the liquid is poured from the bottle counting starts. The first count is not 'one' but 'bubble' and counting should be done at a medium speed.

Count	bubble	2	3	4
Measure in fluid ounces	¼	½	¾	1

Count	5	6	7	8
Measure in fluid ounces	1¼	1½	1¾	2

Stir

Cocktails that call for stirring usually only contain spirits or a spirit and a mixer. By stirring a drink you are able to control the amount of dilution and chill the drink without aerating it whilst keeping the clarity of the liquor. The method of stirring can be applied to basic long drinks with juice that just need to be mixed briefly, and drinks that need chilling. More often though, this method is used for the classics such as Dry Martini, Manhattan, Old Fashioned and Sazerac.

Shake and strain

When shaking a drink always add the ingredients into a clean, odour-free mixing glass, then add ice – although it is usual practice to add the ice first when you are making drinks that contain only spirits (e.g. Martini or Manhattan, see Stir). Wherever possible prepare all drinks in front of the guest, this way the guest can see the action of all the ingredients going into the drink. Then hold the mixing glass with one hand on the base and with your other hand cap the Boston shaker firmly on top of the mixing glass, applying downward pressure and a twisting motion to secure the shaker and the glass together.

Once you have created a complete seal between the shaker and the glass turn the Boston shaker over towards yourself so that the mixing glass is facing over your shoulder and hold the base of the shaker firmly in one hand and the mixing glass in the other. Always ensure that the glass half is on top so that if the seal does break the liquid stays mostly in the shaker and you are less likely to cover the ice dump, and most importantly your guests. If you are left-handed, shake over your left shoulder with the mixing glass in your left hand and vice versa. Shaking should be rhythmic, with the ice travelling the length of the Boston shaker, not simply jumping around from side to side.

Shaking a drink isn't simply the case of giving the shaker a casual wiggle. The amount of time and the strength of the shake will affect the drink's temperature, dilution and consistency.

Some drinks require more dilution than others. Shaking dilutes ice to water, which in turn will soften the alcohol and lengthen the drink. Drinks that require a little more dilution (e.g. Daiquiris) or that contain ingredients that do not mix so easily (such as cream, eggs, fresh fruit or syrups) should be shaken for

about 7 to 15 seconds or until the shaker is frozen on the outside. Drinks that contain ingredients that do not require too much dilution (juices) or mix easily (mixing spirits together) should be shaken for around 3 to 5 seconds or until the outside of the shaker is chilled to the touch.

Shaking is also an expression of your style. Although this may sound a little peculiar, there are hundreds of styles to shaking, which have become almost a signature to modern bartenders. Be sure to shake your drinks with confidence, elbows up, firm stance and try to control your facial expressions!

Once you have shaken the drink, break the seal of the Boston by holding the shaker firmly in one hand, with your index finger supporting the mixing glass and strike the tin firmly, about an inch from the top of the tin, with the heel of your other hand. If it doesn't work the first time move the tin around and try again.

Remove the mixing glass, ensuring not to drip any liquids into the ice dump, then place the strainer on top of the shaker and strain into a glass. Squeeze the strainer against the tin slightly to create a smile in between the shaker and the strainer so the

liquid pours out consistently and smoothly and the shaker retains any large pieces of ice or fruit. If pouring more than one drink be sure to pour out the liquid evenly, adding to each glass gradually.

Finally, clean everything thoroughly and return to their appropriate place.

THE DON'TS OF SHAKING

✘ Never use crushed ice when shaking. (unless more water is required)
✘ Never shake one handed; this can be dangerous and looks unprofessional.
✘ Don't shake with the mixing glass facing the ground or the customer.
✘ Don't over-shake a drink; too much dilution can make a drink bland, flat and watery.
✘ Conversely not shaking a drink properly may not chill the drink enough or mix the ingredients well enough.

Fine (double) strain

If a recipe requires fine straining, use a sieve to double-strain the finer shards of ice and tiny pieces of fruit and seeds.

Muddling

There are literally dozens of muddlers, from the flat end of a bar spoon, rolling pin, or custom-made wooden muddlers to the more authentic stick of sugar cane.

The principle of muddling is to ensure that the ingredients being muddled are crushed properly,

DO'S AND DON'TS OF MUDDLING

✔ Only use a mixing glass, rocks or Collins glass to muddle in.
✔ Ensure that fruit is chopped into pieces small enough to muddle.
✔ When using leaf herbs muddle gently and be sure not to tear them into small pieces.
✔ If muddling in a rocks or Collins glass use a napkin on the top of the glass so as not to handle the top of the glass as the drink will be served in this glass and not transferred to another.
✘ Never muddle in stemmed glassware or slings.
✘ Never muddle liquids of more that 1 ounce, as they may splash out.

releasing the juices, oils and herb aromas, and making sure that all flavours combine. Always use a tall enough muddler so that hands are not touching the glass, and one that is narrow enough to fit the glass. Place the ingredients in the glass and muddle by applying downward pressure and a twisting motion.

Blending

When blending a drink use a commercial blender. Blending produces frozen drinks that contain a lot of ice, which in turn produce a lot of water. Fresh fruit, cream and ice cream drinks all call for blenders. Add the ingredients to the blender with some crushed ice (regular ice can damage the blades), then whiz until the ingredients are completely blended.

Layering

This method is used to form layers in a drink. Each ingredient is carefully poured into the glass so that it floats on the previous layer. Layering is affected by the alcohol and sugar content in the ingredients used: the higher the alcohol content, the lighter the liquid and the higher it will float

in the drink; the higher the sugar content, the heavier the liquid and the lower the liquid will sink.

Layering is required for a number of drinks, most popularly pousse-cafés, and are generally served in 1- or 2-oz shot glasses. Cocktails can also be layered, i.e. layering Champagne on peach purée to make a Bellini.

Both ends of the bar spoon are used for layering. The 'coin' end is used for layering champagne and the spoon end, for layering pousse-cafés. Always pour carefully and consistently, using your finger to cover the air hole to slow down spirits or liqueurs and position the spoon so that it touches the sides of the glass and the liquid.

Flaming

Always take extreme precaution when flaming drinks. If you are lighting a flammable spirit or liqueur you should always use a gas flame, not a petrol (Zippo) flame. When lighting a liquid, make sure the flame touches the liquid and be careful not to burn yourself. Some alcohols, such as Galliano, take a little more time to light and some, like absinthe, light immediately. A general rule of thumb is that the higher the proof/ABV the easier it will be to light.

When flaming a drink that will then be poured it is best to use a brandy balloon or a wine glass. Add the liquor to the glass and swirl it around, coating the inside of the glass with the liquid, then tilt the glass at an angle of approximately 70–80 degrees, so that the liquid is close to pouring out. Light the liquid by touching the flame on the liquid and rotate the glass. Once the liquid is on fire ensure the glass remains tilted and then pour into another glass, keeping a consistent and even pour. Before serving ensure that the flame

is completely out and that the serving glass has cooled down properly.

If the flame goes out, follow the steps again, however, take extreme precaution when lighting as the liquid will flame immediately.

Important safety precautions

- Use a gas flame, not a petrol flame.
- Always warn guests when flaming drinks.
- Do not leave the flamed liquid in the balloon or wine glass for too long as this will cause thermal shock and the glass may shatter.
- When pouring flamed liquid make sure the pour is consistent and poured at an angle of 110–120 degrees to ensure the liquid does not dribble onto your hand.
- Practise, practise and practise some more before you attempt this at the bar.
- Fire should be respected and used with extreme precaution. If you are not 100% confident that you can do this professionally, then practise until you are.

Heat the glass.

Add the liquid and swirl around the glass.

Flame the liquid.

Carefully pour the liquid.

COCKTAILS AND MIXOLOGY

COCKTAILS AND MIXOLOGY

Cocktail-making, or the craft of creating a balanced, visually appealing and palatable drink, lies in the ability to combine flavours. Treat all drinks like a work of art and you will become one step closer to becoming a professional bartender.

HISTORY

It is widely regarded that the first definition of the word 'cocktail' as a type of drink was when a reader allegedly wrote in to a New York newspaper in 1806 enquiring about a previously written recipe of a bittered sling. The editor responded, defining what exactly the newly born cocktail was:

'A cock tail, then, is a stimulating liquor, composed of spirits of any kind, sugar, water and bitters. It is vulgarly called a bittered sling.'

The origins of the word may well precede this date but the important thing to remember is that cocktails, by definition, are over 200 years old and have stood the test of time. Today, cocktails are experiencing a comeback, appearing in TV advertisements, music videos and fashion the world over. To say that cocktails are in vogue would be an understatement, considering that through the ages the cocktail has always been fashionable in one way or another and has reflected changes in taste and culture.

THE STRUCTURE OF THE COCKTAIL

BASE is the term given for the fundamental or distinguishing ingredient used in a cocktail. The base ingredient will generally be one of the spirit categories of vodka, gin, whisky, rum, tequila, brandy and on occasions higher strength liqueurs (30–40%). It is possible to combine two spirits or liqueurs as the base ingredients. Examples of spirits that work well are rye and bourbon whiskies, and tequila and white rum. In the majority of cocktails the base can be substituted for another spirit to make variations. For instance, in an Old Fashioned the original base is bourbon, but aged rum, whisky and other aged spirits can be used in place of the bourbon to make a 'twisted classic'.

MODIFIERS are the ingredients, in combination with the base, which characterise the cocktail and modify the flavours within the drink. Modern drinks predominantly use sweet (sugar syrup) and/or citrus (lemon or lime juice) ingredients to cut through the alcohol and soften or enhance the flavours from the base spirit or liqueur. Other ingredients used to modify a cocktail include fresh fruit,

herbs and spices; aromatised wines and bitters; fruit juices, purées, cordials and syrups; and egg, cream and sugars.

It is advisable to use strong flavours and very sweet/sour ingredients sparingly.

THE SUBSTITUTION THEORY

Also referred to as 'twisted classics' by the modern mixologist. This mixological method takes the base spirit of a cocktail, for instance the bourbon in an Old Fashioned, and substitutes it for another spirit, therefore twisting the original cocktail to produce a 'twisted classic'. The same method and other ingredients usually apply; however, it is wise to adjust the drink to your guest's personal taste. Examples of classic twists are:

Old Fashioned twists:
Replace the bourbon used in the original Old Fashioned to make the following:
Añejo Old Fashioned: aged rum or aged tequila
Whisky Old Fashioned: malt whisky
Cognac Old Fashioned: VSOP or XO cognac

Notice the relationship with the substitution theory. The original classic called for an aged dark spirit, therefore this method and style of drink works for that particular style of spirit; a vodka Old Fashioned wouldn't work in the same way as it doesn't have the same oak characters that combine well with the other ingredients.

Mule twists:
Replace the vodka used in the original Moscow Mule to make the following:
London/Chelsea Mule: London Dry Gin
Scottish Mule: Scotch whisky
Kentucky Mule: bourbon whiskey
Cuban Mule: Cuban rum
Mexican Mule: blanco tequila

Caipirinha twists:
Replace the cachaça used in the original Caipirinha to make the following:
Caipirosca: vodka
Caipirissima: rum
Caipirisky: Scotch whisky
Camparinha: Campari

Collins twists:
Replace the gin used in the original Collins to make the following:
Sandy/Jock Collins: Scotch whisky
Jack Collins: Jack Daniel's whiskey
Pedro Collins: blanco rum

THE MODIFIER THEORY

The modifier theory is based on established classic or contemporary classic drinks with the addition of a sweet or sour element, continuing with the theme of the base spirit or accentuating a particular flavour underlying within the spirit.

Daiquiri – Aged rum
Raspberry Daiquiri
Strawberry and Balsamic Daiquiri
Vanilla Daiquiri

Margarita – Tequila blanco
Passion Fruit Margarita
Pineapple and Pepper Margarita
My Mexican Honey

Caipirinha/Caipirosca – Cachaça/Vodka
Watermelon Caipirinha – Fresh watermelon
Raspberry Caipirosca – Fresh raspberries

Collins – Vodka
Peach Collins – Peach purée
Elderflower Collins – Elderflower cordial

INGREDIENTS

There are three levels of ingredients used when modifying drinks. You should always consider restrictions of availability and cost when selecting appropriate ingredients.

Primary ingredients
Use fresh produce, such as fruit, herbs, spices and vegetables to complement or enhance flavours within a particular spirit, e.g. raspberry with J&B Rare, vanilla with Appleton Extra and lemon with Tanqueray gin. Primary ingredients are generally the most costly and rely on seasonality. Although fresh

ingredients produce the best quality drinks they can be inconsistent and often quite impractical for commercial use in busy bars.

The most practical fresh ingredients to use are freshly squeezed citrus juices, such as lemon, lime and grapefruit. Herbs and spices are generally readily available and if prepared in advance for drinks are practical. For example, if the mint leaves are picked from the stem they can be used quickly and more efficiently.

Secondary ingredients

Syrups, cordials and concentrated juices and purées used as a substitute for the fresh ingredients are generally accepted as the most commercial and practical ingredients to use in cocktails.

Tertiary ingredients

Liqueurs, schnapps and flavoured spirits, such as Bols, Giffard, Joseph Catron, Stolichnaya and Absolut flavoured vodkas.

CREATIVITY, EXPERIMENTATION AND LEARNING

Be bold and don't be afraid to experiment. The majority of foods and drinks we consume today were crafted by experimenting with basic ingredients and learning from the good, the bad and the ugly concoctions. Inspiration for many of the drinks you see in bars today was taken from the classic mixes.

THE SENSORY EXPERIENCE

The experience of a cocktail, when made properly, can tickle all of the senses and give the consumer an amazing sensory experience. Aim to massage the five senses.

Visual: the presentation of the drink, the glass, colour, garnish and how it is made, along with the bartender's style and delivery.

Sound: the sounds created by the bartender making the drink: shaking, pouring, sloshing and the sound of the ice in the glass or the fizz from the drink.

Feel: the temperature of the drink and the feel of the glass in the hand.

Aroma: the aroma of the drink and the garnishes that are used for the drink.

Taste: the mouth-feel, texture, density, sweetness, sourness, bitterness, alcohol, umami, temperature and aftertaste. The mouth contains over 10,000 taste buds and the tongue can only detect five taste sensations: sweet, sour, salt, bitter and umami; everything else we perceive as taste comes from aroma.

COCKTAIL CATEGORIES EXPLAINED

The name, like the garnish and the liquid ingredients, can distinctly help the marketability of a drink and help to promote, identify and categorise the drink for the consumer and bartender, but there is often more to it than that.

Many new cocktails fit well within traditional definitions and many old styles have been forgotten. Conversely, by knowing and understanding classic cocktail categories and methods, beginners as well as seasoned bartenders may well be inspired and the art of mixology will become a lot clearer. Almost every cocktail created in modern bartending has its roots in one of the classics, either by method or ingredients, or has been given a modern twist with an ingredient that wasn't available when first invented.

There was much deliberation about how to categorise the cocktails in this book and with many a note scribbled on a bar napkin the following pages are organised from basic serves to the more complicated cocktail categories. The idea is to practise making the simple drinks exceptionally well and work through the categories, mastering each along the way, along with its variations and twists.

Contemporary and classic favourites have been included in equal measure, as well as those cocktails that, to the traditionalist, are simply dreadful disco drinks. Included in the following pages are the foundations of mastering the art of mixology and the message here is quite clear – get the simple things right and walk before you try to run!

SIMPLE SERVES

The simple serves are just that: very basic drinks such as a juice, soda or spirit served either neat, straight up or on the rocks.

Neat/Straight: the simplest of serves, straight from the bottle to the glass.

Straight up/Classic: this is when a drink has been stirred or shaken with ice and then strained into a Martini glass.

On the rocks/Short: this is generally associated with spirits as in 'whiskey on the rocks'. The drink is served in an ice-filled glass. It can also be shaken then strained over ice, as with the Straight up. Essentially it's a drink on ice.

Long: a term used for drinks served in a long glass over ice.

COCKTAIL RECIPES

There are literally hundreds of thousands of cocktail recipes, using a huge variety of weird and wonderful ingredients. Featured within these pages are just some of the most well-known cocktails served in bars around the world. Every good bartender should have a thorough knowledge of what goes into the most popularly called-for cocktails. It takes a lot of practice to get the mix just right so persevere – the results will be worthwhile.

DRINK NAMES AND FAMILIES

The original names for cocktails have been used throughout where possible, and many of the recipes will explain a story behind the name. The origins of most classic drinks are shrouded in blurred bar talk and folklore, and although the origins of some drinks have several stories, in the end it's a matter of opinion.

The recipes have been grouped into families of drinks, taking into account the ingredients used and the method with which the drink is prepared; some classic recipes have been adapted to modern-day bartending.

GLASSWARE

Always use the size of glass recommended for a particular recipe as each drink is designed for that glass size. There are hundreds of different designs of glassware but make sure you use a durable glass for commercial use.

TYPES OF ICE

When some of the recipes in this guide were conceptualised, ice was made and used differently, from chipping away at a large block of ice with an ice pick, to shaving ice and smashing chunks with an ice axe. Thankfully today we have commercial ice-makers which produce all shapes, sizes and densities of ice.

Ice is a vital ingredient in the preparation and presentation of cocktails. Before you attempt to make great drinks you should ensure you have a plentiful supply of quality solid cubed ice. Some ice machines produce slated or hollow ice cubes and these are not suitable as they melt too quickly.

Where crushed ice is recommended, be sure to use freshly crushed ice (snow ice), not slushy (wet) crushed ice that has been sitting at the bottom of an ice dump as this will dilute a drink too quickly. The type of ice recommended for each recipe is important to the final taste, texture, temperature and presentation. The golden rule for using ice is to never use ice twice, unless stated.

RECIPES

The ingredients used in the following recipes have been adapted for modern bartending and are available behind most bars the world over. Where the original ingredients are not available modern substitutes have been used instead. For all drinks the ingredients have been listed in the order they should be used.

Where a recipe calls for fresh ingredients or freshly squeezed juice do not compromise or substitute these ingredients, as the final drink will vary dramatically.

An asterisk next to the name of a drink means the recipe has been devised by the author.

GARNISHES

Always use the best quality fruit, herbs and spices available to dress a drink. Cocktails should be visually appealing and a simple rule to apply to garnishing drinks is to always try to use an ingredient that is present in the drink (i.e. a lime wedge for a daiquiri, lemon peel to complement the citrus undertones of some vodkas, and orange peel with Cointreau for instance).

ALLERGIES

Please note that some drinks may contain nuts, dairy or wheat and if you or any of your customers have allergies, take extreme precaution when preparing or consuming mixed drinks.

HIGHBALLS

A highball is a tall drink that contains a single spirit and a carbonated mixer (soda, tonic, cola, diet cola, ginger ale, ginger beer or bitter lemon) served on cubed ice in a Collins glass. There are hundreds of highball variations. Here are a few points to remember when preparing and serving any long drink:

- Always use a clean, solid, 12 oz glass, chilled if possible.
- Use cubed ice, and lots of it. The glass should always be full of ice. This will keep the glass cold for longer and slow dilution.
- Use a quality spirit.
- Use a quality mixer.
- If you're going to use fruit to garnish the drink use a decent size piece of freshly cut fruit, no blemishes, stickers or dirt.

BUCK

Bucks can be made with all spirit categories including, vodka, gin, whisky, tequila, rum and originally brandy, and take their name from the spirit used. Variations of this drink get their names from the spirit being used, for example Whisky Buck, Brandy Buck, Bourbon Buck.

Glass: 12 oz Collins
Method: build
Recipe
Ice cubes
2 oz chosen spirit
Top with ginger ale
2 lime wedges

Fill the glass with ice and add your chosen spirit. Top with ginger ale and stir. Squeeze one of the lime wedges into the glass and discard. Garnish with the remaining lime wedge. Serve with a long straw.

HORSE'S NECK

The Horse's Neck dates back to the beginning of the 20th century and is defined by the horse's neck garnish that hangs off the side of the glass. An interesting mix of ingredients with bourbon being preferred for a popular modern-day version.

Glass: 12 oz Collins
Method: build
Recipe
Ice cubes
2 oz brandy or bourbon
Top with ginger ale
Lemon spiral or horse's neck, to garnish

Fill the glass with ice and add the brandy or bourbon. Top with ginger ale and stir. Garnish with the lemon spiral or horse's neck. Serve with a long straw.

OTHER POPULAR HIGHBALLS WITH CARBONATES:
PRESBYTERIAN (Scotch whisky + soda)
DARK 'N' STORMY (Gosling's rum + ginger beer)
CANADIAN (rye whisky + ginger ale)

GIN AND TONIC

Gin and Tonic, or G&T as it's widely known, is the quintessential English drink, and has been part of British heritage for well over a hundred years.

Glass: 12 oz Collins

Method: build

Recipe

Ice cubes

2 oz gin

Top with tonic water

Lime wedge

Lime wedge or lemon slice, to garnish

Fill the glass with ice and add the gin. Top with tonic and stir. Squeeze a wedge of lime into the glass and rub the lime around the rim, then discard. Garnish with a wedge of lime or slice of lemon. Serve with a long straw.

OTHER POPULAR HIGHBALLS WITH TONIC:

HENDRICKS GIN AND TONIC (garnish with a thick slice of cucumber)

VODKA AND TONIC (garnish with a lemon slice)

TEQUILA AND TONIC (garnish with a lime wedge)

BAILIE NICOL JARVIE WHISKY AND TONIC (AKA THE BLT) (garnish with a lime wedge)

PINK GIN AND TONIC (add a dash of Angostura bitters for the colour and flavour)

Clear spirits tend to work better with tonic, with the exception of some whiskies, including Bailie Nicol Jarvie. Drinks that don't work with tonic are liqueurs, most notably Baileys, Amaretto, Frangelico and other such nut or cream liqueurs.

GIN RICKEY

The base of the drink is always a spirit with the addition of lime and soda water, and it is always served long. The name for the Rickey is rumoured to have came from Colonel Rickey, an English officer based in Washington D.C. This is a great alternative to G&T, having a more sour edge and without the bitterness of the tonic.

Glass: 12 oz Collins

Method: build

Recipe

Ice cubes

2 oz gin

1 oz lime cordial or fresh lime juice

Soda water

Lime wedge, to garnish

Fill the glass with ice and add the gin and lime cordial or juice. Top with soda and stir. Garnish with a wedge of lime. Serve with a long straw.

VODKA RICKEY

Although the traditional name for this drink is the Vodka Rickey, this drink is generally ordered as a 'Vodka, lime and soda'.

Glass: 12 oz Collins

Method: build

Recipe

Ice cubes

2 oz vodka

1 oz lime cordial or fresh lime juice

Soda water

Lime wedge, to garnish

Fill the glass with ice and add the vodka. Most people prefer lime cordial instead of fresh lime – it's always best to ask. Top with soda and stir. Squeeze a wedge of lime into the glass. Serve with a long straw.

Variations of this simple and refreshing drink get their names from the spirit taking the place of the vodka, for example Rum Rickey, Whisky Rickey, etc. Soda water is used with most spirits as a lengthener, softening the alcohol content and adding an effervescence. The most popular serves are whisky and soda, and vodka and soda. Lemonade is also used as a lengthener for spirits and liqueurs, including vodka and Archers (peach schnapps).

CUBA LIBRE

The Cuba Libre is a simple yet superbly refreshing drink and just like many of the highballs it has very little history to go with it. Lore has it that Cuba Libre was the chant and cheer of the American soldiers after liberating Cuba from the rule of the Spanish. Cuba Libre translates as Free Cuba.

Glass: 12 oz Collins

Method: build

Recipe

Lime wedge

Ice cubes

2 oz rum

Cola

Lime wedge, to garnish

Squeeze a lime wedge into the glass. Rub the lime around the rim of the glass and discard. Fill the glass with ice and add the rum. Top with cola and stir. Garnish with a wedge of lime. Serve with a long straw.

Try using different styles and ages of rum to make this drink: lighter rums add freshness and tend to taste more alcoholic whereas aged rums add caramel, chocolate, spice and smoothness to the drink. A simple substitution of ginger beer for the coke makes a Dark 'n' Stormy, which really enhances the spice and flavour of the rum. If possible use fiery Jamaican ginger beer.

OTHER POPULAR HIGHBALLS WITH COLA:

VODKA AND COLA (garnish with a lemon slice)

BOURBON AND COLA (garnish with an orange slice)

SAILOR JERRY AND COLA (garnish with a lime wedge)

JACK DANIEL'S AND COLA – aka **JD & COKE** (no garnish)

SCOTCH AND COLA (no garnish)

TEQUILA AND COLA (garnish with a lime wedge)

SOUTHERN COMFORT AND COLA – aka **SOCO** (garnish with an orange twist)

TIA MARIA AND COLA (garnish with a maraschino cherry)

MALIBU AND COLA (no garnish)

PIMM'S CUP – AKA PIMM'S AND LEMONADE

Pimm's was invented in 1823 by James Pimm, a farmer's son from Kent who subsequently became the owner of an oyster bar in the City of London. For an interesting alternative top with champagne instead of lemonade for a Pimm's Royale.

Glass: 12 oz sling 12 oz Collins

Method: build

Recipe

Ice cubes

Lemon slice

Orange slice

Cucumber slices

½ strawberry, sliced

6 mint leaves plus extra, to garnish

2 oz Pimm's No 1

Lemonade (Schweppes is preferred)

Cucumber slice, strawberry and mint sprig, to garnish

Fill the glass with ice and add all the fruit slices and mint leaves to the glass. Add the Pimm's and top with lemonade. Stir gently with a long straw to mix the ingredients. Garnish with a slice of cucumber, a strawberry and a sprig of mint.

COCKTAILS WITH JUICE

There are hundreds of mixed drinks that can be made using a single spirit and/or liqueur and fruit juices; here are a few of the most popular international mixes.

SCREWDRIVER

The name Screwdriver supposedly came around in the 1950s when American oil workers were stationed in the Middle East and mixed vodka and canned orange juice, stirred with whatever came to hand, generally a screwdriver, hence the name.

Glass: 12 oz Collins

Method: shake & strain

Recipe

2 oz vodka

4 oz fresh orange juice

Ice cubes

Orange wheel or slice, to garnish

Add the vodka and orange juice into a mixing glass and fill with ice. Cap with a Boston shaker and shake vigorously for a few seconds. Strain into an ice-filled glass. Garnish with an orange wheel or slice. Serve with a long straw.

VARIATIONS:

TETANKA (Zubrowka vodka + apple juice)

FREDDIE FUDPUCKER (tequila + orange juice)

HARVEY WALLBANGER

The story of how this drink came about is an intriguing one. Apparently a surfer named Harvey used to consume vast amounts of Screwdrivers with a Galliano float after a hard day's surfing. A fair few cocktails later he would pick up his board and attempt to leave. Walking out of a bar with a surfboard is hard at the best of times, and Harvey would stumble out bouncing off the walls, hence the name Harvey Wallbanger.

Glass: 12 oz Collins

Method: build & shake

Recipe

1½ oz vodka

Fresh orange juice

Ice cubes

½ shot Galliano

Orange wheel or slice, to garnish

Add the vodka and orange juice into a mixing glass and fill with ice. Cap with a Boston shaker and shake vigorously for a few seconds. Strain into an ice-filled glass, then float the Galliano on the top. Garnish with an orange wheel or slice. Serve with a long straw.

TEQUILA SUNRISE

This drink is in essence a Freddie Fudpucker with grenadine.

Glass: 12 oz Collins

Method: shake & strain

Recipe

2 oz tequila blanco

Fresh orange juice

Ice cubes

¼ oz grenadine

Orange wheel or slice, to garnish

Add the tequila and orange juice into a mixing glass and fill with ice. Cap with a Boston shaker and shake vigorously for a few seconds. Strain into an ice-filled glass. Drizzle the grenadine slowly down the inside of the glass. Garnish with an orange wheel or slice. Serve with a long straw.

CAPE COD

This drink is named after the popular holiday resort in Massachusetts. Essentially a vodka and cranberry juice, this drink has become very popular, having similar bitter/dry characteristics to a gin and tonic. For those who don't like gin, the Cape Cod is an alternative that comprises berry freshness and a dry edge without the distinctive gin overtones.

Glass: 12 oz Collins

Method: shake & strain

Recipe

2 lime wedges (one to garnish)

2 oz vodka

Cranberry juice

Ice cubes

Squeeze a wedge of lime into a mixing glass. Add the vodka and cranberry juice and fill with ice. Cap with a Boston shaker and shake vigorously for a few seconds. Strain into an ice-filled glass. Garnish with a wedge of lime and serve with a along straw.

Simple additions of another fruit juice make a Breeze, the most famous of Breezes is the Sea Breeze, with the addition of grapefruit juice. Adding spirits or liqueurs expands the category further to drinks like the Woo Woo, Cosmopolitan and Sex on the Beach.

As with most fruity cocktails shaking the drink will result in a much more chilled and better tasting drink, but they are commonly built and stirred for speed and efficiency in busier bars.

SEA BREEZE

The dry ingredients give a wonderful freshness to this classic summer cocktail. Some say a Sea Breeze is a Cape Cod with grapefruit juice, some say it's a Greyhound with cranberry juice. A Greyhound is a vodka and grapefruit juice; adding a salt rim makes it a Salty Dog.

Glass: 12 oz Collins
Method: shake & strain
Recipe
Ice cubes
2 lime wedges
2 oz vodka
2 oz cranberry juice
2 oz grapefruit juice

Put the ice into a mixing glass and squeeze one wedge of lime into the glass. Add the vodka, cranberry and grapefruit juices, and cap with a Boston shaker. Shake vigorously for a few seconds and pour into a Collins glass. Garnish with a lime wedge.

You can also add the cranberry juice to an ice-filled Collins glass. Place the remaining ingredients in a Boston shaker, shake for a few seconds then pour carefully over the cranberry, creating a white layer over the cranberry. Garnish with a fresh wedge of lime and serve with a long straw.

VARIATIONS:

The Breeze category is a range of cocktails that all have vodka, cranberry and lime but also contain another fruit juice.

SUMMER/BAY BREEZE (pineapple)
AUTUMN/WINTER BREEZE (apple)
MEDITERRANEAN BREEZE – aka the **MADRAS** (orange)
CARIBBEAN BREEZE (mango)
ORIENTAL BREEZE (lychee)

SEX ON THE BEACH

Love it or hate it, this is probably one of the most well known cocktails of recent times, and one that has been changed and twisted time and again. A summer fruit punch cocktail, the fruity ingredients enable this drink to be enjoyed by young and old. The recipe may change slightly depending on where you are; here are a couple of variations.

Sex on the Beach I

Glass: 12 oz Collins
Method: shake & strain
Recipe
Ice cubes
1 oz vodka
1 oz peach schnapps
3½ oz fresh orange juice
Drizzle of grenadine
Lime wedge, to garnish

Put the ice into a mixing glass and add the vodka, peach schnapps and orange juice. Cap with a Boston shaker and shake vigorously for a few seconds. Strain into an ice-filled glass and drizzle the grenadine over the drink. Garnish with a wedge of lime. Serve with a long straw.

Sex on the Beach II

Glass: 12 oz Collins
Method: shake and strain
Recipe
2 lime wedges
1½ oz vodka
½ oz Chambord
1½ oz cranberry juice
1½ oz pineapple juice
Ice cubes

Squeeze one wedge of lime into a mixing glass. Add the vodka, Chambord, cranberry and pineapple juices and fill with ice. Cap with a Boston shaker and shake vigorously for a few seconds. Strain into an ice-filled glass, add the second wedge of lime and serve with a long straw.

BLOODY MARY

This is one of the most famous cocktails in the world and is a great drink when made correctly, and one of the worst when not. This drink is often altered or themed depending on where it's served or who it's served to. Hundreds of ingredients can be used to personalise it, from sake and wasabi to beef bouillon and port.

Glass: 12 oz Collins

Method: build & shake

Recipe

2 oz vodka

Fresh tomato juice

Salt and pepper

Worcestershire sauce

Tabasco sauce

Dash of lemon or lime juice

Ice cubes

Lime or lemon wedge, to garnish

Add the vodka, tomato juice and condiments to a mixing glass and fill with ice. Cap with a Boston shaker and shake gently, then pour back into the glass. This drink should have a thick soup-like consistency, so shake the ingredients gently so as not to dilute the mix. Garnish with a wedge of lime or lemon. Serve with a long straw.

Other garnish variations include rimming the glass with celery salt and adding a stick of celery as a stirrer; floating a little sherry on top; or adding a little cracked pepper.

VARIATIONS:

BLOODY MARIA (substitute vodka for tequila).

BLOODY MARY-LOU (substitute vodka for bourbon).

RED SNAPPER (substitute vodka for gin).

BLOODY MED (muddle basil and green olives in the bottom of a Collins before building the Bloody Mary. Also works well with tequila and bourbon).

BLOODY MARY BUFFET (this includes a tray of spices, herbs, condiments, sauces, aperitifs and wines that can be added to the base ingredients of the Bloody Mary to create a personalised version. Here, the customer decides which condiments they would like).

BLOODY CAESAR (substitute tomato juice for clamato juice – a tomato juice with clam flavourings).

SANGRITA

Sangrita is a traditional popular Mexican drink that is usually served as a sipping shot with a shot of tequila. The following will make four single shots of Sangrita.

Glass: Shot glass

Method: shake & strain

Recipe

2 oz tomato juice

⅔ oz fresh orange juice

⅓ oz lime juice

⅓ oz grenadine

Tabasco sauce, to taste

Coarse salt

Ice cubes

Ground black pepper,
   to garnish

Shot of tequila

Add all the ingredients into a mixing glass and fill with ice. Cap with a Boston shaker and shake for a few seconds. Strain into four shot glasses and serve with shots of tequila. Garnish with a dash of freshly ground black pepper.

CLASSICS

Classic cocktails are those drinks that have stood the test of time and were first created well over 50 years ago. This section takes you through the most popular classics that the modern bartender should master before even attempting to whip up their own fancy concoctions.

COLLINS

The Collins family is principally an extensive range of fresh lemonades with alcohol. The key to successfully making these recipes is the ability to balance the tart sourness with the sweetness of the sugar and the strength of the alcohol used. The carbonate then adds an effervescent texture and helps draw out some of the intense flavours.

TOM COLLINS

This drink is credited to Mr John Collins, a bartender at the Limmer's hotel in London in the 1800s. The drink was christened the Tom Collins, taking its name partly from the bartender and from the use of Old Tom gin. The sister of the Collins is the Fizz, which is a short Collins with charged water (from a soda siphon) and ungarnished. Add egg white to make a Silver Fizz; add the yolk and it becomes a Golden Fizz. Although this drink was originally made by building the ingredients in an ice-filled glass, this recipe calls for shaking.

Glass: 12 oz Collins

Method: shake & strain

Recipe

2 oz London Dry Gin

1 oz lemon juice

1 oz sugar syrup

Ice cubes

Soda water

Lemon wheel or wedge,
   to garnish

Add the gin, lemon juice and sugar syrup into a mixing glass and fill with ice. Cap with a Boston shaker and shake for a few seconds. Strain into an ice-filled glass and top with soda. Garnish with a lemon wheel or wedge. Serve with a long straw. Some bartenders also like to add a cocktail cherry for a classic look.

THE COLLINS FAMILY:

The method of making a Collins is all-important. This five S's system will help you make the perfect Collins every time:

S – SPIRIT Almost all spirits can be used as a substitute for the original gin. These include Scotch, Bourbon, rum, tequila, cachaça or cognac.

S – SWEET Other than granulated sugar or sugar syrup, the sweet element to this drink can be modified using other flavoured syrups, purées, fresh fruit*, liqueurs and cordials. (* Note the sweetness of fresh fruit will vary depending on the season so you will need to add a small amount of sugar syrup to draw out the natural sweetness of the fruit.)

S – SOUR The sour element of the drink can be changed for lime juice, bitter orange juice, grapefruit or pink grapefruit juice. Always use freshly squeezed juice where possible.

S – SHAKE Shake vigorously and strain into an iced-filled Collins glass.

S – SODA A Collins requires a certain effervescence, however other carbonates can be used. If using a sweetened carbonate (cola) be sure to reduce the amount of sweet element in the recipe to counter-balance the drink.

COLLINS VARIATIONS

There is a multitude of variations of this cocktail, all made with simple substitution of the base spirit, sweet or sour element. If the base spirit in this drink is changed, then the name also changes. For instance:

Sandy/Jock Collins (Scotch whisky)
Michael Collins (Irish whiskey)
Colonel Collins (bourbon whiskey)
Jack Collins (Jack Daniel's whiskey)
Pedro Collins (blanco rum)
Jose Collins (blanco tequila)
Pierre Collins (VS cognac)

To ensure that the drink is balanced it is important to adjust the amount of sugar used for aged spirits as there will be a certain level of sweetness already from the vanillin from the wood ageing process i.e. some aged rums and bourbons.

NOTE: You can also add fruit, purées, cordials, syrups and/or liqueurs to the standard recipe. When modifying a recipe, be sure to balance the flavours of sweet and sour, and ensure the ratio of spirit, sour, sweet and lengthener is maintained.

MODIFIED VARIATIONS

JERRY COLLINS

This is a great twist on the original Collins, using a spiced rum with vanilla notes. Always adjust the sweetness to taste. If a spiced rum is not available, flavour your own light rum by adding a couple of split vanilla pods.

Glass: 12 oz Collins glass

Method: shake & strain

Recipe

2 oz Sailor Jerry's spiced rum (Captain Morgan's spiced rum or Kweyol spiced rum)

1 oz lemon juice

¼ oz vanilla syrup (adjust to taste)

Ice cubes

Soda water

Lemon slice or wedge, to garnish

Add the rum, lemon juice and vanilla syrup into a mixing glass and fill with ice. Cap with a Boston shaker and shake for a few seconds. Strain into an ice-filled glass and top with soda. Garnish with a wedge or slice of lemon. Serve with a long straw.

CUCUMBER COLLINS

Hendricks gin burst onto the bar scene in recent years from Ayrshire, Scotland, and is now being used in some exciting twists on classic drinks including this little number. The rose and cucumber flavours work well in this long summer drink.

Glass: 12 oz Collins or 12 oz sling

Method: shake & strain

Recipe

2 oz Hendricks gin

1 oz lemon juice

½ oz sugar syrup

3 cucumber slices

Ice cubes

Soda water

Lemon slice or wedge and cucumber slice, to garnish

Add the gin, lemon juice, sugar syrup and cucumber into a mixing glass and fill with ice. Cap with a Boston shaker and shake for a few seconds. Strain into an ice-filled glass and top with soda. Garnish with a lemon slice or wedge and a slice of cucumber. Serve with a long straw.

ELDERFLOWER COLLINS

A British summer favourite, the fresh floral sweetness of elderflower cordial works well in combination with the sour of fresh lemons. Use apple juice to lengthen this drink as an alternative to or in combination with soda.

Glass: 12 oz Collins or 12 oz sling

Method: shake & strain

Recipe

2 oz gin

1 oz lemon juice

½ oz elderflower cordial

¼ oz sugar syrup

Ice cubes

Soda water or apple juice

Lemon slice or wedge, to garnish

Add the gin, lemon juice, cordial and sugar syrup into a mixing glass and fill with ice. Cap with a Boston shaker and shake for a few seconds. Strain into an ice-filled glass and top with soda or apple juice. Garnish with a lemon slice or wedge. Serve with a long straw.

BERRY COLLINS (AKA RASPBERRY COLLINS, BLACKBERRY COLLINS, BLACKCURRANT COLLINS, STRAWBERRY COLLINS, BLUEBERRY COLLINS)

There are literally hundreds of twists to the classic version of the Collins and with a little imagination and creativity you can create a myriad of Berry Collins by combining different fruits and by adding complementary sweeteners, such as honey and vanilla.

Glass: 12 oz Collins

Method: shake & strain

Recipe

2 oz vodka

1 oz lemon juice

1 oz berry purée, or ½ oz berry syrup/liqueur

¼ oz sugar syrup (adjust to taste)

Ice cubes

Soda water

Lemon slice and berry, or lemon and berry sail, to garnish

Add the vodka, lemon juice, purée and sugar syrup into a mixing glass and fill with ice. Cap with a Boston shaker and shake for a few seconds. Fine-strain into an ice-filled glass and top with soda. Garnish with a slice of lemon and a berry. Serve with a long straw.

HONEY BERRY COLLINS

A popular contemporary twist on the Collins combines sweet berry flavours with the sweetness of honey. If Krupnik honey vodka is not available balance the drink by adding a little honey syrup.

Glass: 12 oz Collins

Method: shake & strain

Recipe

2 oz Krupnik honey vodka

1 oz lemon juice

1 oz raspberry purée, or ½ oz raspberry syrup or Chambord or raspberry liqueur

Honey syrup (adjust to taste)

Crushed ice

Soda water

Lemon wheel or wedge and raspberry filled with runny honey, to garnish

Add the vodka, lemon juice, purée and honey syrup into a mixing glass and fill with ice. Cap with a Boston shaker and shake for a few seconds. Fine-strain into an ice-filled glass and top with soda. Garnish with a lemon wheel or wedge and a honey-filled raspberry. Serve with a long straw.

LONG ISLAND ICE TEA

This is the original ice tea cocktail and is credited to Robert (Rosebud) Butt in 1976 at the Oka Beach Inn, Long Island. Although it contains five spirits they should only be present in small amounts. The drink is about the blend of liquor, not the strength, and should look like tea, and not a long glass of cola.

Glass: 12 oz Collins

Method: shake & strain

Recipe

½ oz vodka

½ oz white rum

½ oz triple sec

¼ oz gin

¼ oz tequila

1 oz fresh lemon or lime juice

½ oz sugar syrup

Ice cubes

Cola

Lemon or lime slice or wedge, to garnish

Add the vodka, rum, triple sec, gin, tequila, lemon or lime juice and sugar syrup into a mixing glass and fill with ice. Cap with a Boston shaker and shake for a few seconds. Strain into an ice-filled glass and top with cola. Garnish with a slice/wedge of lemon or lime (or both). Serve with a long straw.

VARIATIONS:

The sugar syrup in the Long Island can be substituted for other flavours, so experiment with matching flavours.

LONG BEACH ICE TEA (substitute cola for cranberry juice)

KENTUCKY ICE TEA (substitute triple sec for Kentucky bourbon)

TENNESSEE ICE TEA (substitute triple sec for Jack Daniels)

SPICED ICE TEA (substitute triple sec for spiced rum)

TOKYO ICE TEA (substitute gin for Midori and use lemonade instead of cola)

ATLANTIC ICE TEA (substitute cola for lemonade and the triple sec for blue curaçao)

BEVERLY HILLS ICE TEA (substitute cola for champagne and serve in a champagne glass)

OLD FASHIONED

Commonly referred to as the bartender's cocktail, the bourbon Old Fashioned originated in the early 1900s and is a landmark in cocktail lore. Over time this drink has remained quite consistent with only slight changes. These changes generally require the addition of a piece or two of fruit – either a maraschino cherry or a slice of orange. This cocktail takes about 5 to 7 minutes to prepare.

Glass: 10 oz Old Fashioned or Rocks

Method: build and stir

Recipe

2 barspoons demerara sugar

2 dashes of Angostura bitters

2 oz bourbon

Ice cubes

Orange peel, to garnish

Add the sugar, bitters and ⅓ oz of bourbon into an old fashioned glass. Stir for 1 minute with the flat end of a barspoon to dissolve the sugar and blend the bitters and bourbon. Add 1 ice cube and stir for another minute. Continue the gradual dilution by adding 1 oz bourbon and 2 more ice cubes, and stir for 2 minutes. Add the remaining bourbon and 2 more ice cubes, and stir for a further 2 minutes. Garnish by spraying the oil of an orange peel over the drink, twist and place into the drink. A more traditional garnish is an orange slice and a maraschino cherry.

OLD FASHIONED VARIATIONS

AÑEJO/RUM OLD FASHIONED (substitute bourbon for aged rum)

AÑEJO/TEQUILA OLD FASHIONED (substitute bourbon for aged tequila)

CACHAÇA (BRAZILIAN) OLD FASHIONED (substitute bourbon for aged cachaça)

BRANDY OLD FASHIONED (substitute bourbon for brandy)

WHISKY OLD FASHIONED (substitute bourbon for malt or Scotch blended. This can be done with the majority of Scotch whiskies. Be sure to experiment – it can be a lot of fun!)

MODIFIED OLD FASHIONS (AKA NEW FASHIONS)

The foundations of these drinks can be adapted to create some fantastic classic twists by substituting the sugar, bitters and/or adding subtle flavours to complement that of the spirit being used.

*TALISKER RE-FASHIONED

This is a modern take on the classic Old Fashioned, using the same method to prepare the drink and the smoky spicy characters of an Islay whisky. The spicy notes in the Benedictine and cordial combine with the smoky spice of Talisker. The amount of sugar used can be adjusted to taste.

Glass: 10 oz Old Fashioned

Method: stirring/gradual dilution

Recipe

1½ barspoons demerara sugar

3 dashes of Peychaud's bitters

⅓ oz Bottlegreen spiced berry cordial

10 ml Benedictine

2 oz Talisker 10 Year Old Whisky

Ice cubes

1 cinnamon stick, to garnish

Add the sugar, bitters, cordial, Benedictine and ⅓ oz of Talisker into an old fashioned glass. Stir for 1 minute with a barspoon to dissolve the sugar and blend the ingredients, then add 1 ice cube and stir for another minute. Continue the gradual dilution by adding ⅔ oz Talisker and 2 more ice cubes, and stir for 2 minutes. Add the remaining ounce of Talisker and 2 more ice cubes. Now stir for 2 minutes with the cracked cinnamon stick (instead of the barspoon) to impart some of the spice from the cinnamon. Leave the cinnamon stick in the drink as a garnish.

CAIPIRINHA

This is a traditional cocktail from Brazil, also known as 'Peasant's Drink'. The Caipirinha is a very intense drink containing a whole lime, sugar and spirit. The original spirit used in this cocktail is Cachaça.

Glass: 10 oz rocks

Method: muddle

Recipe

1 lime cut into 6 wedges

2 barspoons demerara sugar or 1 oz demerara sugar syrup

Crushed ice

2 oz Cachaça

Dice the lime wedges and place in a rocks glass. Pour over the sugar or syrup and muddle with a large muddler. Fill the glass with crushed ice, add the Cachaça and stir. No garnish is required for this drink as the lime remains in the glass.

VARIATION

FRUIT CAIPIRINHA

For a fruit Caipi, add fresh fruit during the muddling stage and reduce the amount of fresh lime used. Berry fruits are preferred although grapes, peaches and pears all work well. The ease with which this drink can be modified makes it popular among bartenders and customers alike.

Glass: 10 oz rocks

Method: muddle

Recipe

3 lime wedges

1 oz fruit purée or equivalent muddled fresh fruit

2 barspoons of granulated sugar or 1 oz sugar syrup

Crushed ice

2 oz spirit (cachaça, vodka, rum or whisky)

Appropriate garnish

Dice the lime wedges and place in a rocks glass with the fruit. Pour over the sugar or syrup and muddle with a large muddler. Fill the glass with crushed ice, add the spirit of choice and stir. Garnish with appropriate fruit.

MINT JULEP

This drink's name is derived from the Arabic word 'julab', meaning rose water, and was famously served at the Kentucky Derby at the turn of the 1800s.

Glass: 12 oz Collins

Method: muddle & stir

Recipe

12–16 large mint leaves (adjust to taste)

½–1 oz demerara sugar syrup or 1–2 barspoons of demerara sugar

Dash of Angostura bitters

Crushed ice

2 oz bourbon

Mint sprig, to garnish

Add the mint leaves, sugar and bitters into a Collins glass and muddle lightly with a barspoon. Fill the glass with crushed ice and pour in the bourbon. Rapidly raise and lower the spoon to thoroughly mix the drink. Garnish with a sprig of mint, rubbing the leaves gently before serving to release the bouquet.

VARIATIONS

The classic julep can be twisted by adding fresh fruit or purée during the muddling stage. By using the substitution and modifier theory there are dozens of exciting variations; try an original version with brandy, rum or rye whisky. Popular modern variations include the Mango Julep, Peach or Cherry Julep.

MOJITO

The Mojito has its origins in the 17th century when Admiral Francis Drake of the British Navy offered sailors a mixture of mint and rum to eliminate stomach and respiratory problems. This drink also has its roots in the deep-south favourite, the Julep. Rumour has it that Americans holidaying away from Prohibition wanted a Julep-style drink so the Cuban bartenders used the local rum, lengthened with soda and lime, and the Mojito was born.

Glass: 12 oz Collins

Method: muddle, build & stir

Recipe

2–4 lime wedges

½ oz–1 oz demerara sugar syrup or 1–2 barspoons demerara sugar (adjust to taste)

8–16 large mint leaves (adjust to taste)

Crushed ice

2 oz light or aged rum

Soda water

Mint sprig

Add the lime and sugar into a Collins glass and muddle. Add the mint leaves and place the flat end of the barspoon in the glass. Fill the glass with crushed ice and pour in the rum. Rapidly raise and lower the spoon to thoroughly mix the drink, then top with soda. Garnish with a sprig of mint, rubbing the leaves before serving to release the bouquet.

FRUIT MOJITOS

Just like many other drinks in this book the original Mojito can be altered with fruit or purée at the muddling stage or by substituting the spirits and sodas. A Mojito should be a light, long refreshing drink and not a really flavour-heavy cocktail. However, some people will prefer more sugar, mint or lime and some will like more of everything.

NEED-TO-KNOW CLASSICS

Here are some of the need-to-know classic drinks that have stood the test of time. Here we pay homage to all those drinks that modern bartenders should know.

AMERICANO

The predecessor to the Negroni, the Americano was originally created in Gaspare Campari's bar in the 1860s. Originally known as the Milano-Torino, taking the name from the origins of the two ingredients – Campari from Milan and Cinzano from Turin. The name was then changed to the Americano when it was made popular by American tourists visiting Italy during the Prohibition era.

Glass: 10 oz rocks

Method: build & stir

Recipe

1 oz Cinzano or sweet vermouth

1 oz Campari

Ice cubes

Soda water

Orange slice, to garnish

Add the Cinzano and Campari to an ice-filled rocks glass and top with soda water. Garnish with a slice of orange.

NEGRONI

Although the jury is still out on the origins of this drink, it is believed that it was Count Camillo Negroni who asked the bartender at the Casoni bar in Florence in 1919 for a splash of gin in his Americano. This drink is a classic aperitif, with a dry bitterness and a spicy sweetness which comes from the Cinzano.

Glass: 10 oz rocks

Method: build & stir

Recipe

1 oz gin

1 oz Cinzano or sweet vermouth

1 oz Campari

Ice cubes

Orange slice, to garnish

Add the gin, Cinzano and Campari to an ice-filled rocks glass. Garnish with a slice of orange.

SAZERAC

It is widely believed that the Sazerac was first invented in the mid 1850s by Antoine Amédée Peychaud (inventor of Peychaud's bitters) and Sewell Taylor at his coffee house in New Orleans. Most probably named after the popular brand of cognac, Sazerac-du-Forge et fils.
A dash of absinthe was also added by Leon Lamothe, which adapted this drink to what we know today. This cocktail made its film debut in the James Bond film Live and Let Die.

Glass: 10 oz rocks

Method: in/out

Recipe

10 ml absinthe

2 oz rye whisky (or cognac)

Dash of Peychaud's bitters

5 ml sugar syrup

Lemon or orange twist, to garnish (optional)

Fill a rocks glass with absinthe and chilled water. Swirl around the glass to coat the inside, then discard. Add the whisky, bitters and sugar syrup to a separate mixing glass, stir, and strain into the chilled rocks glass. Garnish with a lemon or orange twist.

VARIATIONS

Try substituting Chartreuse, Benedictine, Jägermeister or any other herbal liqueur for the absinthe.

SINGAPORE SLING

Some credit the creation of this classic to Ngiam Tong Boon a bartender working at the Long bar in the Raffles Hotel in Singapore around 1910–15. However, the recipe was not documented until 1922 in Robert Vermiere's *Cocktails and How to Mix Them*, although it was named the Straits Sling and doesn't mention that the recipe comes from the Raffles Hotel. The first printed recipe of the Singapore Sling was in the 1930 *Savoy Cocktail Book* by Harry Craddock. Robert Vermiere's version of the recipe is given below, along with the modern version served at the Raffles Hotel.

STRAIT SLING – ROBERT VERMIERE'S VERSION

This is the original version taken from Robert Vermiere's 1922 book *Cocktails and How to Mix Them*. Although this drink was first served in a tumbler, a sling glass has been used here.

Glass: 11 oz sling

Method: build & stir

Recipe

2 dashes of Angostura bitters

2 dashes of orange bitters

½ oz lemon juice

½ oz Benedictine

½ oz dry cherry brandy

2 oz gin

Soda water

Pineapple slice and maraschino cherry, to garnish

Add all the ingredients into a sling and top with soda. Garnish with a slice of pineapple and a maraschino cherry.

RAFFLES HOTEL VERSION

This is the modern version of the Singapore Sling on the 2007 menu at the Raffles Hotel.

Glass: 14 oz sling

Method: build & stir

Recipe

30 ml gin

15 ml cherry liqueur

10 ml Benedictine

10 ml Cointreau

10 ml grenadine

25 ml lemon juice

60 ml pineapple juice

Dash of Angostura bitters

Soda water

Slice of pineapple and maraschino cherry, to garnish

Add all the ingredients into an ice-filled sling glass, top with soda and stir. Garnish with a pineapple slice and a maraschino cherry.

SOURS

One of the all-time classic cocktails dating back to the mid 1800s and a very versatile drink as it can be made with any spirit. The addition of egg white helps to gel the ingredients in the drink and also leaves a smooth foam across the surface. A small dash of pineapple juice is often used in substitution for egg white.

WHISKEY SOUR

The original Whiskey or Brandy Sours, and indeed any sour made with a dark or aged spirit, can sometimes benefit from a dash of orgeat (almond syrup) to deepen the flavours.

Glass: 10 oz rocks

Method: shake & strain

Recipe

2 oz bourbon whiskey

1 oz lemon juice

1 oz sugar syrup

4 drops of Angostura bitters

1 tsp egg white (a dash of pineapple juice can replace the egg white)

Ice cubes

Lemon twist, to garnish

Add all the ingredients into a mixing glass and fill with ice. Cap with a Boston shaker and shake vigorously to create a foamy drink. Strain into an ice-filled glass. Spray the oils from the lemon peel over the drink and tuck the twist into the foam. Serve with two sip straws.

MIDORI SOUR

Using liqueurs to make a sour produces a distinctly different drink than if using spirits. Midori is a honeydew melon-flavoured liqueur that is quite sweet so it is best to either omit the sugar altogether or add a small amount to taste.

Glass: 10 oz rocks

Method: shake & strain

Recipe

2 oz Midori

1 oz lemon juice

Sugar syrup (adjust to taste, maximum ½ oz)

Dash of pineapple juice

Ice cubes

Lemon twist, to garnish

Add all the ingredients into a mixing glass and fill with ice. Cap with a Boston shaker and shake vigorously to create a foamy drink. Strain into an ice-filled glass. Spray the oils from the lemon peel over the drink and tuck the twist into the foam. Serve with two sip straws.

VARIATIONS:

Like the Collins, this is a good example of a drink that can be twisted, substituting the base or modifying the other ingredients. The spirit, sour, sugar syrup and bitters can all be changed and with a little imagination and an understanding of flavours and balance a bartender could make literally hundreds of variations.

Popular spirit variations are the Gin Sour, Brandy Sour, Scotch Sour, Rum Sour (much better with aged rum), Pisco Sour and the relatively new Cachaça Sour. Liqueurs that work really well in a sour cocktail are the Midori Sour, Tuscan Sour (using the Italian liqueur Tuaca), Benedictine Sour, Drambuie Sour, Amaretto Sour and Amaretto Stone Sour (with the addition of orange juice). When making a sour with sweeter spirits and liqueurs the sugar syrup should be reduced to ensure a balanced drink, and the bitters are generally omitted.

AMARETTO SOUR

Amaretto is an almond/marzipan flavoured liqueur with a high sugar content so it is recommended to either omit the sugar altogether or add a small amount to taste, similarly to the Midori Sour.

Glass: 10 oz rocks

Method: shake & strain

Recipe

2 oz amaretto

1 oz lemon juice

Sugar syrup (adjust to taste)

Dash of pineapple juice

Ice cubes

Dash of Angostura bitters

Lemon twist, to garnish

Add all the ingredients into a mixing glass and fill with ice. Cap with a Boston shaker and shake vigorously to create a foamy drink. Strain into an ice-filled glass and add a dash of Angostura bitters. Spray the oils from the lemon peel over the drink and tuck the twist into the foam. Serve with two sip straws.

HONEY BERRY SOUR

The honey and berry combination works well as a variation for many classic drinks such as the Collins, Mule, Daiquiri and Margarita, although raspberry is the most common variation. Other berries, such as blackberry, blueberry and strawberry work well here.

Glass: 10 oz rocks

Method: shake & strain

Recipe

1 oz vodka

½ oz Chambord or raspberry liqueur

1 oz lemon juice

½ oz honey syrup

1 tsp egg white (a dash of pineapple juice can replace the egg white)

Ice cubes

Lemon twist, to garnish

Add all the ingredients into a mixing glass and fill with ice. Cap with a Boston shaker and shake vigorously to create a foamy drink. Strain into an ice-filled glass. Spray the oils from the lemon peel over the drink and tuck the twist into the foam. Serve with two sip straws.

GRAPEFRUIT AND HONEY SOUR

Be sure to use freshly squeezed grapefruit juice in this recipe and not lemon juice. This recipe works particularly well if using Beefeater gin, to complement the grapefruit undertones of this particular gin.

Glass: 10 oz rocks

Method: shake & strain

Recipe

2 oz gin

1 oz fresh grapefruit juice

½ oz honey syrup

¼ oz sugar syrup (adjust to taste)

2 drops of Angostura bitters

1 tsp egg white (a dash of pineapple juice can replace the egg white)

Ice cubes

Grapefruit twist, to garnish

Add all the ingredients into a mixing glass and fill with ice. Cap with a Boston shaker and shake vigorously to create a foamy drink. Strain into an ice-filled glass. Spray the oils from the grapefruit peel over the drink and tuck the twist into the foam. Serve with two sip straws.

BRAMBLE

Created by Dick Bradsell in the mid-1980s at Fred's Club, London. Although not strictly a sour this is a modern version of a sour.

Glass: 10 oz rocks

Method: shake & strain

Recipe

2 oz gin (originally Bombay Sapphire)

1½ oz lemon juice

½ oz sugar syrup

Crushed ice

½ oz crème de mure (blackberry liqueur)

Lemon twist and blackberry, to garnish

Add the gin, lemon juice and sugar syrup into a mixing glass and fill with ice. Cap with a Boston shaker and shake vigorously. Strain into a crushed ice-filled glass. Drizzle crème de mure over the top and spray the oils from the lemon peel over the drink. Garnish with a lemon twist and blackberry. Serve with two sip straws.

RAMOS FIZZ

Created in 1888 by Henrico C Ramos in the Imperial Cabinet Saloon in New Orleans. It was originally called a New Orleans Fizz. Ramos insisted each drink be shaken for at least 10 minutes and hired shaker boys to whip up these drinks, shaking the drink until their arms hurt before passing it down the line to the next.

Glass: 10 oz rocks

Method: shake & strain

Recipe

2 oz gin

½ oz lime juice

½ oz lemon juice

½ oz sugar syrup

½ oz single cream

½ barspoon of orange flower water

½ egg white

Ice cubes

Soda water

Lemon and lime shavings, to garnish

Put all the ingredients (minus the soda) into a mixing glass and fill with ice. Cap with a Boston shaker and shake for a few minutes. Strain into an ice-filled glass and top with soda. Garnish with lemon and lime shavings. Serve with two sip straws.

MULES

The original mule was the Moscow Mule and was created in 1941 by Jack Martin (a sales representative of the company who acquired the rights for Smirnoff in the US) and Jack Morgan (who was struggling to sell a large order of ginger beer). This drink launched the international success of Smirnoff vodka and to promote the new cocktail copper mugs were made with a kicking mule on them that celebrities of the time had their names engraved on.

MOSCOW MULE

The original mule called for Smirnoff vodka, however, most standard and premium vodkas can be used for this drink. Fresh lime juice is essential here.

Glass: 12 oz Collins

Method: shake & strain

Recipe

2 oz vodka

½ oz lime juice

¼ oz sugar syrup

Dash of Angostura bitters

Ice cubes

Ginger beer

Lime wedge, to garnish

Add the vodka, lime juice, sugar syrup and bitters into a mixing glass and fill with ice. Cap with a Boston shaker and shake. Strain into an ice-filled glass and top with ginger beer. Garnish with a wedge of lime. Serve with a long straw.

RASPBERRY MULE

Glass: 12 oz Collins

Method: shake & strain

Recipe

1½ oz vodka

½ oz fresh fruit purée/liqueur/flavoured syrup

½ oz fresh lime juice

¼ oz sugar syrup

Dash of Angostura bitters

Ice cubes

Ginger beer

Lime wedge, to garnish

Add the vodka, fruit purée, lime juice, sugar syrup and bitters into a mixing glass and fill with ice. Cap with a Boston shaker and shake for a few seconds. Strain into an ice-filled glass and top with ginger beer. Garnish with a wedge of lime. Serve with a long straw.

JÄGERMEISTER MULE

A Jäger Mule offers an unusual variation using the German bittersweet medicinal flavoured liqueur made from 56 varieties of herbs, fruits and spices. Benedictine can be used in place of Jägermeister.

Glass: 12 oz Collins

Method: shake & strain

Recipe

1 oz vodka

½ oz lime juice

¼ oz sugar syrup

Dash of Angostura bitters

Ice cubes

Ginger beer

1 oz Jägermeister

Lime wedge, to garnish

Add the vodka, lime juice, sugar syrup and bitters into a mixing glass and fill with ice. Cap with a Boston shaker and shake. Strain into an ice-filled glass and top with ginger beer and Jägermeister. Garnish with a wedge of lime. Serve with a long straw.

DAIQUIRIS

It is generally accepted that the American engineer Jennings Cox first invented the daiquiri, working near Daiquiri in Cuba. It is believed that in 1896 when entertaining some VIPs, Cox ran out of his gin supply so offered his guests a local mixture of rum and lemon juice and added granulated sugar as the drink was too harsh. This simple classic was made famous in the 1950s by President John F. Kennedy who proclaimed it to be his favourite cocktail.

VARIATIONS

Rum, fresh lime and sugar should be present in all daiquiris, however, the use of different rums will affect the style of the drink. Lighter rums inject a fresh/rawness whereas aged rums bring a deeper, smoother and chocolaty character. Warmer climates generally serve frozen daiquiris blended with strawberries or bananas. The more popular contemporary twists of the Daiquiri tend to use subtle variations, keeping the rum and lime but using a different sweetener, enhancing the subtle flavours and undertones of a particular rum.

CLASSIC DAIQUIRI

The daiquiri is the perfect rum-savouring cocktail as the sugar and lime take the harsh edge off the rum and enhance the flavour, bringing the caramels and spices to the forefront. Here is a modern version of the classic, where lime is commonly used in place of lemon, and sugar syrup in place of granulated sugar.

Glass: 10 oz rocks or 5 oz Martini

Method: shake & fine-strain

Recipe

2 oz aged rum

½ oz lime juice

1 barspoon of sugar syrup

Ice cubes

Lime wedge, to garnish

Add all the ingredients into a mixing glass and fill with ice. Cap with a Boston shaker and shake vigorously until the shaker freezes on the outside. Strain into an ice-filled glass or fine-strain into a chilled Martini glass. Garnish with a wedge of lime. To serve on the rocks, strain over ice in a rocks glass.

STRAWBERRY AND BALSAMIC DAIQUIRI

This is a popular modern twist to the classic Daiquiri combining sweet and savoury flavours to produce a strangely delicious drink.

Glass: 5 oz Martini

Method: shake & fine-strain

Recipe

2 oz aged rum

½ oz lime juice

½ oz strawberry purée or equivalent muddled fresh strawberries

¼ oz aged balsamic vinegar

1 barspoon of sugar syrup

Ice cubes

½ strawberry and balsamic reduction, to garnish

Add all the ingredients into a mixing glass and fill with ice. Cap with a Boston shaker and shake vigorously until the shaker freezes on the outside. Fine-strain into a chilled glass. Garnish with half a strawberry and a drop of balsamic reduction. Balsamic reduction can be made by adding balsamic vinegar to a saucepan and boiling with demerara sugar, until it reduces to a thick, sticky liquid. It can also be purchased.

VANILLA/CINNAMON/CARAMEL/ HONEY DAIQUIRI

Flavoured syrups offer a modern variation of this classic drink and complement the flavours present in some aged rums.

Glass: 5 oz Martini

Method: shake & strain

Recipe

2 oz blanco or aged rum

½ oz lime juice

⅓ oz vanilla/cinnamon/caramel or honey syrup

Ice cubes

Appropriate garnish

Add all the ingredients into a mixing glass and fill with ice. Cap with a Boston shaker and shake vigorously until the shaker freezes on the outside. Fine-strain straight up into a chilled Martini glass. The garnish should complement your chosen flavoured syrup.

FRUIT DAIQUIRI

For the best fruit daiquiris use a quality purée or fresh fruit. There are hundreds of fruit flavours and combinations that work with rum, so experiment with flavours and try combining fruit flavours with spices.

Glass: 5 oz Martini

Method: shake & strain

Recipe

2 oz blanco rum

½ oz lime juice

½ oz fruit purée, 10 ml liqueur or equivalent muddled fresh fruit

1 barspoon of sugar syrup

Ice cubes

Lime wedge, to garnish

Add all the ingredients into a mixing glass and fill with ice. Cap with a Boston shaker and shake vigorously until the shaker freezes on the outside. Fine-strain into a chilled Martini glass. Garnish with an appropriate fresh fruit garnish.

BACARDI COCKTAIL

The Bacardi Cocktail is a version of the Daiquiri made with grenadine and in 1936 a New York court ruled that this drink could only be made with Bacardi rum, making it the world's first trademarked cocktail.

Glass: 5 oz Martini

Method: shake & strain

Recipe

2 oz Bacardi carta blanca

1 oz lime juice

½ oz sugar syrup

1 barspoon of grenadine syrup

Ice cubes

Lime wedge, to garnish

Add all the ingredients into a mixing glass and fill with ice. Cap with a Boston shaker and shake vigorously until the shaker freezes on the outside. Fine-strain straight up into a chilled Martini glass. Garnish with a 'perky' lime wedge.

SIDECAR

Similar to the Daiquiri in its basic form, it is widely documented that the Sidecar was first invented by bartender Harry at Harry's New York Bar in Paris after World War I and named after a motorcycle sidecar in which an army captain was chauffeur-driven to and from the bar. However, in Harry's own book he credits the invention of the drink to Mac Garry of the Bucksclub in London.

Glass: 5 oz Martini

Method: shake & fine-strain

Recipe

1½ oz VS cognac

1 oz Cointreau

1 oz lemon juice

Ice cubes

Lemon knot, to garnish

Add all the ingredients into a mixing glass and fill with ice. Cap with a Boston shaker and shake for a few seconds. Fine-strain into a chilled glass. Sugar-coat the rim for a touch of glamour and garnish with a lemon knot.

BETWEEN THE SHEETS

This drink's background has been lost in history, however, this classic mix does resemble that of a Daiquiri and Sidecar combined.

Glass: 5 oz Martini

Method: shake & fine-strain

Recipe

1½ oz VS cognac

½ oz blanco rum

½ oz Cointreau

1 oz lemon juice

½ oz sugar syrup

Ice cubes

Lemon twist, to garnish

Add all the ingredients into a mixing glass and fill with ice. Cap with a Boston shaker and shake for a few seconds. Fine-strain into a chilled glass. Spray the oils from the lemon peel over the drink and drop into the glass. Sugar-coat the rim if you like.

MARGARITA

The Margarita, meaning daisy in Spanish, was supposedly created in 1946 by Margarita Sames at a cocktail party in Acapulco in Mexico. If using blanco instead of aged tequila, add a little more sugar.

Glass: 10 oz rocks or 5 oz Martini

Method: shake & strain

Recipe

1¼ oz tequila

¾ oz Cointreau/triple sec/Grand Marnier

1 oz lime juice

1 barspoon of sugar/agave syrup

Ice cubes

Lime wedge or wheel, to garnish

Add all the ingredients into a mixing glass and fill with ice. Cap with a Boston shaker and shake for a few seconds. Strain over an ice-filled rocks glass or fine-strain chilled into a Martini glass that has been frosted with salt (optional). Garnish with a 'perky' lime wedge or lime wheel.

PASSION FRUIT MARGARITA

A popular variation of this drink using passion fruit purée or liqueur. The bittersweet flavours combine well with the tequila and lime.

Glass: 10 oz rocks or 5 oz Martini

Method: shake & strain

Recipe

1½ oz tequila

½ oz Cointreau

½ oz passion fruit purée or Passoã (passion fruit liqueur)

½ oz sugar/agave syrup

1 barspoon of lime juice

Ice cubes

½ passion fruit or lime wedge, to garnish

Add all the ingredients into a mixing glass and fill with ice. Cap with a Boston shaker and shake for a few seconds. Strain into an ice-filled rocks glass or fine-strain chilled into a Martini glass that has been frosted with salt. Garnish with the passion fruit or lime wedge.

MARGARITA VARIATIONS

A classic twist on the margarita is the Japanese Slipper, which substitutes a melon liqueur for the Cointreau. The Margarita can be twisted similarly to the Daiquiri, using fresh fruit, purées, syrups or liqueurs. Also using rested and aged tequilas can change the dimension of this classic tequila cocktail.

*PINEAPPLE AND BLACK PEPPER MARGARITA (AKA P&P MARGARITA)

The sweet fluffy texture of pineapple combines unusually well with ground black pepper. Using fresh pineapple is preferred, however pineapple purée and juice can also be used.

Glass: 7 oz margarita

Method: shake & fine-strain

Recipe

1½ oz tequila

½ oz triple sec

1 oz fresh pineapple puree or (muddled fresh pineapple chunks)

1 barspoon of lime juice

1 barspoon of sugar syrup

Plenty of ground black pepper

Ice cubes

⅛ pineapple slice, to garnish

Add all the ingredients into a mixing glass and fill with ice. Cap with a Boston shaker and shake vigorously for 10 seconds. Fine-strain into a chilled glass that has been half rimmed with ground black pepper. Garnish with a pineapple slice and a small grind of pepper.

*MY MEXICAN HONEY

This drink was created to showcase the flavours of reposado tequila. The use of fresh honeydew melon and honey add a velvety smooth finish to the drink. Although not strictly a Margarita this is a modern twist on a Margarita.

Glass: 5 oz Martini

Method: shake & fine-strain

Recipe

1½ oz reposado tequila

1 oz fresh honeydew melon purée

⅓ oz lime juice

1 barspoon of honey syrup (adjust to taste)

1 barspoon of vanilla syrup (adjust to taste)

Ice cubes

Honeydew melon slice, to garnish

Add all the ingredients into a mixing glass and fill with ice. Cap with a Boston shaker and shake for a few seconds. Fine-strain into a chilled glass. Garnish with a slice of melon.

MARTINIS

This category aims to give you an overview of this visually simple yet complex creation. There are literally hundreds of ways to make a Martini and thousands of variations put forward by contemporary mixologists. Here is a list of those recipes that have stood the test of time, along with some interesting modern variations and methodologies.

MARTINEZ COCKTAIL

It is thought the modern version of the Dry Martini originated as a variation of the Martinez made by Julio Richelieu in the late 1800s. Back then it was a wineglass of Italian sweet vermouth and a pony (1 oz) of gin. Nobody really knows how it transformed into a teardrop of dry vermouth in an ocean of gin.

Glass: 5 oz Martini

Method: shake & strain

Recipe

Dash of Boker's bitters

2 dashes of maraschino

½ oz Old Tom gin

2 oz Italian vermouth

Ice cubes

¼ lemon slice, to garnish

Sugar syrup (optional)

Add all the ingredients into a mixing glass and fill with ice. Cap with a Boston shaker and shake for a few seconds. Strain into a glass. Garnish with a thin slice of lemon. If the guest prefers the drink very sweet, add two dashes of sugar syrup.

DRY MARTINI

Martini di Arma di Taggia (in 1912 at the Knickerbocker Hotel in New York) is the bartender generally credited with the modern Dry Martini. It was him that paired London dry gin and vermouth with a dash of bitters. The original recipes were vermouth-heavy and French vermouth wasn't available until the late 1890s, so Italian vermouth is generally regarded as the original.

Glass: 5 oz Martini

Method: see Methodologies of the Dry Martini, below

Recipe

Up to 15 ml Italian vermouth

2 oz gin or vodka

Garnish: popular garnishes include either a lemon twist for vodka and citrusy gins, or an olive on a cocktail stick, generally used with gin.

METHODOLOGIES OF THE DRY MARTINI

There are literally hundreds of subtle variations for preparing this classic drink and you may find that modern bartenders have their own way of preparing this drink.

1) Pour vermouth into an ice-filled mixing glass. Stir 10 to 15 times, strain and discard excess vermouth. Add the gin or vodka to the glass, stir 10 to 15 times, and strain into a chilled Martini glass.

2) Pour vermouth directly into a Martini glass and swirl around. Add the gin or vodka into an ice-filled mixing glass, stir 10 to 15 times and strain into the Martini glass.

3) Atomise or spray vermouth on to the inside of a Martini glass. Add the gin or vodka into an ice-filled mixing glass, stir 10 to 15 times, strain into the Martini glass.

4) Add frozen gin or vodka into a frozen/chilled Martini glass, and then pour a couple of drops of vermouth onto surface.

VARIATIONS ON VERMOUTH CONTENT

Bone Dry or Extra Extra Dry Martini: no vermouth, just 2 oz stirred gin or vodka

Extra Dry Martini: dash of dry vermouth stirred with 2 oz gin or vodka

Dry Martini: 1 barspoon of dry vermouth, stirred with 2 oz gin or vodka

Slightly Wet Martini: ⅓ oz dry vermouth, stirred with 2 oz gin or vodka

Wet Martini: 15 ml dry vermouth stirred with 2 oz gin or vodka

Perfect Martini: 2.5 ml dry vermouth and 2.5 ml sweet vermouth, stirred with 2 oz gin or vodka

Sweet Martini: 5 ml dry vermouth, stirred with 2 oz gin or vodka

VARIATIONS ON GARNISH

Naked Martini: no ice, all ingredients straight from the freezer, very strong, no garnish

Gibson Martini: garnished with two silver-skin/cocktail onions. This name is taken from the infamous 'Gibson Girls' of America, who were, to say the least, 'top heavy'

Dickens Martini: made traditionally but with no garnish

Franklin Martini: garnish with two green olives. This name is taken from the American President Roosevelt and is how he liked his Martini

Dean Martin: served with three green olives, just how the legend himself liked to drink it

MODIFIED VARIATIONS

Dirty Martini: add 1 teaspoon of olive brine to the original recipe

Filthy Martini: add ½ oz olive brine to the original recipe

Saketini: replace the gin or vodka with sake rice wine

Vesper Martini: 1½ oz vodka, ½ oz gin, 5 ml Lillet Blonde vermouth, shaken NOT stirred. Garnish with an orange peel

FLAVOURED MARTINIS

Flavoured Martinis have no real resemblance to the classic Dry Martini; they generally use a vodka or gin base and are served in a Martini glass and the relationship stops there. Here are some popular modern Martini:

FRESH FRUIT MARTINIS

Most fruits can be used in fruit Martinis, with the exception of bananas. Berries and tropical fruits are the most commonly used in Martinis.

Glass: 5 oz Martini

Method: shake & fine-strain

Recipe

1 oz fruit purée or equivalent muddled fresh fruit

2 oz vodka

5 ml sugar syrup

Ice cubes

Appropriate fruit garnish

Muddle the fruit or add the purée to a mixing glass. Add the remaining ingredients and fill with ice. Cap with a Boston shaker and shake vigorously. Fine-strain into a chilled glass. Garnish with the appropriate fruit garnish.

WOO WOO

The tongue in cheek saying about this drink is that 'it's so good they named it twice'. Really though, this drink is as basic as fruit flavoured martinis go. Hardly a classic creation but one you should know nonetheless.

Glass: 5 oz Martini or 10 oz rocks
Method: shake & strain
Recipe

1 oz vodka

1 oz peach schnapps

1 oz cranberry juice

Ice cubes

Lime wedges

Add the vodka, peach schnapps and cranberry juice into a mixing glass and fill with ice. Cap with a Boston shaker and shake vigorously for a few seconds. Fine-strain into a chilled glass. Squeeze a wedge of lime into the glass, then rub it around the rim and discard. You can also build this drink in a rocks glass or serve long by adding more cranberry juice. Garnish with a wedge of lime.

COSMOPOLITAN

The Cosmopolitan has been around, in various guises, since the 1980s. It's one of the most commonly ordered cocktails but this relatively straightforward drink is now more famous for its garnish than its name.

Glass: 5 oz Martini or 10 oz rocks glass
Method: shake & strain
Recipe

1 oz citron vodka

1 oz triple sec or Cointreau

1 oz cranberry juice

Juice of 1 lime wedge

Ice cubes

Add the vodka, triple sec or Cointreau, cranberry and lime juices into a mixing glass and fill with ice. Cap with a Boston shaker and shake vigorously for a few seconds. Double-strain into a chilled glass or serve on the rocks.

Garnish

This drink probably became world famous due to its unique garnish – the orange flambé (see page 44). Cut a thin strip of peel from an orange, taking as little of the pith as possible. Holding the skin towards the drink, snap the peel over a lighter flame. The flame should brush the surface of the drink and the warm oils should spray over the surface, creating an instant aroma and flavour. Wipe the peel around the rim and slip into the drink.

COSMOPOLITAN VARIATIONS

There are a number of variations with both short and long versions.

FRUIT COSMOS: add fresh fruit; berries work very well, particularly raspberries

METROPOLITAN: use Absolut Kurrant vodka instead of citron vodka

PURPLE COSMO: use blue curaçao instead of Cointreau

WHITE COSMO: use white cranberry juice instead of the usual red juice

BASIL GRANDE

Accredited to Jamie Wilkinson, Living Room UK, this cocktail beautifully combines the sweetness of strawberries and raspberries with the dryness of cranberry and herbaceous aroma and flavour of basil, with a spicy kick from the black pepper garnish. This drink helped influence some of the modern combinations of flavoured Martinis.

Glass: 5 oz Martini

Method: muddle, shake & fine-strain

Recipe

½ oz strawberry purée or 4 muddled strawberries

4–6 basil leaves

1 oz vodka

½ oz Chambord

½ oz Grand Marnier

1 oz cranberry juice

Basil leaf and black pepper, to garnish

Muddle the purée or fruit and basil in a mixing glass, add remaining ingredients and fill with ice. Cap with a Boston shaker and shake vigorously. Fine-strain into a chilled glass. Garnish with a basil leaf and a grind of black pepper.

BREAKFAST MARTINI

Created by Salvatore Calabrese at the Library Bar, London, and is a variation of the original Marmalade Martini by Harry Craddock.

Glass: 5 oz Martini

Method: shake & fine-strain

Recipe

1⅔ oz gin

½ oz Cointreau

½ oz fresh lemon juice

1 tsp medium-cut orange marmalade

Ice cubes

Orange spiral, to garnish

Add the gin, Cointreau, lemon juice and marmalade into a mixing glass and fill with ice. Cap with a Boston shaker and shake vigorously. Fine-strain into a chilled glass. Garnish with an orange spiral.

CUCUMBER MARTINI

A refreshing alternative to fruit Martinis and a great palate cleanser and pre-dinner drink.

Glass: 5 oz Martini

Method: muddle, shake & fine-strain

Recipe

2.5 cm (1 in) peeled cucumber

2 oz cucumber vodka or Hendrick's gin

5 ml dry vermouth

Ice cubes

Cucumber slice or cucumber fan, to garnish

Muddle the cucumber in a mixing glass, add the remaining ingredients and fill with ice. Cap with a Boston shaker and shake. Fine-strain into a chilled glass. Garnish with a slice of cucumber or a cucumber fan.

*DISTINCTIVELY BOTANICAL

Designed to complement the botanicals used in Tanqueray gin, juniper being the most predominant flavour and coriander the second. The selected ingredients were used to help lift the flavours already present in the spirit, giving a powerful botanical freshness. The juniper berries can be replaced with homemade juniper sugar syrup.

Glass: 5 oz Martini

Method: muddle, shake & fine-strain

Recipe

20–25 dried juniper berries

6–8 fresh coriander leaves

4–6 fresh mint leaves

1 lime wedge

2 oz Tanqueray gin

½ oz sugar syrup

Ice cubes

Mint or coriander sprig and 2 juniper berries, to garnish

Muddle the juniper berries, coriander, mint and lime in a mixing glass, add the remaining ingredients and fill with ice. Cap with a Boston shaker and shake vigorously for a few seconds. Fine-strain into a chilled glass. Garnish with a mint/coriander sprig and a couple of juniper berries.

ESPRESSO MARTINI

Also known as the Espresso Cocktail or the Vodka Espresso. A superb dessert drink and a personal favourite, which should be made to the customer's taste. As with a regular coffee some will prefer only a little sugar, so be sure to ask.

Glass: 5 oz Martini

Method: shake & fine-strain

Recipe

1 oz vodka

1 ½ oz espresso

1 oz coffee liqueur (Kahlua is preferred)

Ice cubes

Edible coffee beans, to garnish

Chocolate or cinnamon powder (optional)

Add all ingredients into a mixing glass and fill with ice. Cap with a Boston shaker and shake vigorously. Fine-strain into a chilled glass. Garnish with three edible coffee beans and an optional dusting of chocolate or cinnamon powder.

FRENCH MARTINI

A wonderfully sweet and fluffy drink named after the origins of Chambord, the French liqueur used. This drink should be shaken thoroughly so that a fluffy head is formed.

Glass: 5 oz Martini

Method: shake & fine-strain

Recipe

1½ oz vodka

½ oz Chambord or raspberry liqueur

1 oz pineapple juice

Ice cubes

Raspberry, to garnish

Add all the ingredients into a mixing glass and fill with ice. Cap with a Boston shaker and shake vigorously. Fine-strain into a chilled glass. Garnish with a raspberry.

PASS THE DUTCHIE

Created by Zack Foley, the elderflower and cucumber combination creates a wonderfully balanced spring drink.

Glass: 5 oz Martini

Method: shake and fine-strain

Recipe

2.5 cm (1 in) cucumber, peeled

2 oz vodka

½ oz (Dutchie) elderflower cordial

½ barspoon of honey syrup

½ barspoon lemon juice

Lime zest

Cucumber stick or fan, to garnish

Muddle the cucumber in a mixing glass, add the remaining ingredients and fill with ice. Cap with a Boston shaker and shake vigorously for a few seconds. Fine-strain into a chilled glass. Garnish with a cucumber stick or fan.

MANHATTAN

This drink was created at the Manhattan Club for Lady Randolph Churchill, the American society beauty and mother of Winston Churchill. There are a number of accepted variations of the Manhattan, the most popular being the Rob Roy, which was made with Scotch whisky and named after a broadway show. Another is the Harvard that substitutes whisky for brandy or cognac. If applejack or calvados is used it becomes a Star Cocktail.

CLASSIC MANHATTAN

When looking at the recipe you can see that it is closely related to the Martini cocktail, in terms of the ratios and methods used to build it. Just remember that the Manhattan is a red cocktail, the vermouth is generally sweet and it uses whisky and bitters, all of which are red or reddish brown in colour. The garnish, usually a maraschino cherry, is also red. This drink is quite robust and uses strong flavoured ingredients, therefore it is very popular shaken to give added dilution and served on the rocks.

Glass: 5 oz Martini

Method: muddle, shake & strain

Recipe

2 maraschino cherries and 1 orange slice (optional)

½ oz sweet vermouth

2 oz rye whisky or bourbon

Dash of Angostura bitters

1 barspoon of maraschino syrup

Ice cubes

Maraschino cherry and/or orange slice, to garnish

Muddle the cherries and orange slice in a mixing glass, add the remaining ingredients and fill with ice. Cap with a Boston shaker and shake vigorously. Fine-strain into a chilled glass. Garnish with a maraschino cherry and/or slice of orange.

STIRRED MANHATTAN

Using the same ingredients and quantities as the Classic Manhattan, pour the vermouth into an ice-filled mixing glass and stir 10 to 15 times. Add the whisky, bitters and maraschino and stir 10 to 15 times. Strain into a chilled Martini glass. Garnish with a maraschino cherry and/or a peel of orange.

SHAKEN MANHATTAN

Using the same ingredients and quantities as the Classic Manhattan, add all the ingredients to a mixing glass and fill with ice. Cap with a Boston shaker and shake vigorously for a few seconds. Strain into a chilled Martini glass, or serve on the rocks in a rocks glass. Garnish with a maraschino cherry and/or a slice of orange.

PERFECT MANHATTAN

Not technically a perfect drink but the name sake comes from combining both dry and sweet vermouth.

Glass: 5 oz Martini

Method: stir & fine-strain

Recipe

¼ oz sweet vermouth

¼ oz dry vermouth

Ice cubes

2 oz rye whiskey or bourbon

Dash of Angostura bitters

5 ml maraschino syrup

Add the sweet and dry vermouths into a mixing glass, fill with ice and stir 10 to 15 times. Add the whiskey or bourbon, bitters and maraschino syrup. Stir another 10 to 15 times and fine-strain into a chilled glass. No garnish, just perfect!

*THYME FOR JOHNNIE

A modern take on the Rob Roy, replacing the dry bitterness of vermouth with limoncello and adding the spicy notes of ginger and lemongrass, and the floral aromas of lemon thyme to complement the flavours of Johnnie Walker.

Glass: 5 oz Martini

Method: stir and fine-strain

Recipe

⅓ oz Limoncello

⅓ oz Bottlegreen ginger and lemongrass cordial

2 stalks of fresh lemon thyme

1⅓ oz Johnnie Walker 12 Year Old whisky

Lemon thyme stalk, to garnish

Ice cubes

Add the limoncello, cordial and thyme into a mixing glass and stir with one ice cube for about one minute or until the cube is half its size. Add the whisky, a little more ice and stir for another minute. Fine-strain into a chilled glass. Garnish with a stalk of lemon thyme.

CHAMPAGNE COCKTAILS

Here are some of the most popular classic and modern champagne cocktail recipes. Use a good quality house champagne or prosecco instead of an expensive brand. Top quality champagne is best drunk undiluted!

BELLINI

The Bellini is accredited to Giuseppe Cipriani, the head bartender at Harry's Bar in Venice, between 1934 and 1948. It is believed that his inspiration came from the colour of the toga of a saint in a painting by 15th-century Venetian artist Giovanni Bellini.

Glass: 6–8 oz champagne flute

Method: build and layer

Recipe

20 ml white peach purée

Dash of sugar syrup (adjust to taste)

Top with Prosecco (original version) or champagne (modern version)

Slice of white peach, to garnish (optional)

Add the purée and sugar into a champagne flute. Pour the Prosecco or Champagne slowly down the length of a barspoon over the purée to layer. Garnish with a slice of white peach.

VARIATIONS

Popular variations include substituting the peach for strawberry to make a Rossini. Other fresh berry purées, such as blackberries, blueberries and blackcurrants, work equally well.

CLASSIC CHAMPAGNE COCKTAIL

The origins of this drink can be traced back to Jerry Thomas' bon vivants companion of 1862. However, the modern version and recipe we know today was created in 1899, from the winner of a New York cocktail competition.

Glass: 6–8 oz champagne flute

Method: build

Recipe

1 demerara sugar cube

Dash of Angostura bitters

½ oz VS cognac

Champagne

Orange or lemon twist, to garnish

Place the sugar cube on a napkin over the glass and add a dash of bitters to soak the sugar, then drop the sugar cube into the glass. Add the cognac and top with Champagne. Spray the oils of an orange or lemon twist into the drink, then garnish by sliding the twist into the glass.

FRENCH 75

Named after the famous French World War I artillery piece, the 75 mm Howitzer, and said to have been originally concocted by the World War I flying ace Raoul Lufbery. Legend has it that he liked Champagne, but wanted something with a little more kick to it, so he mixed it with gin. The combination was said to have such a kick that it felt like being shelled by the gun of its namesake.

Glass: 6–8 oz champagne flute

Method: build

Recipe

1 oz gin

½ oz lemon juice

10 ml sugar syrup

Ice cubes

Champagne

Lemon spiral and maraschino cherry, to garnish

Add the gin, lemon juice and syrup into a mixing glass with ice. Cap with a Boston shaker and shake for a few seconds. Strain into a Champagne flute. Top with Champagne. Garnish with a lemon spiral and a cherry.

VARIATIONS

Substitute the gin for vodka to make a French 76 or add VS cognac in place of gin to make a French 95.

AFTER DINNER DRINKS

After dinner drinks, also referred to as dessert drinks, are exactly that, drinks that are generally best served after dinner.

BLACK RUSSIAN

Some say there should be a 2:1 ratio between the vodka and coffee liqueur, others say they should be served in equal quantities. Most bartenders will serve this drink in a rocks glass over ice but it can also be served in a Martini glass. The original recipe contained just the two spirits but as tastes have changed the addition of cola has become standard, however, I feel the guest should be given the choice, 'with or without'.

Glass: 10 oz rocks

Method: build & stir

Recipe

Ice cubes

1 oz vodka

1 oz coffee liqueur

Cola (optional)

Cocktail cherry,
   to garnish

Add the vodka, coffee liqueur and optional cola to an ice-filled rocks glass. Garnish with a cocktail cherry.

Common variants include the White Russian, substituting the coke for single cream.

A White or Black Russian with a dash of amaretto becomes a Toasted White or Toasted Black Russian. This can then be turned into an Orgasm by adding Bailey's and from there dozens of variations.

BRANDY ALEXANDER

Popular during Prohibition in the United States, it is believed that the original version was made with bathtub gin (named Alexander) and cream to mask the flavour of the poorly made crude alcohol.

Glass: 5 oz Martini

Method: shake & fine-strain

Recipe

1½ oz cognac

¾ oz crème de cacao

1 oz double cream

Ice cubes

Grated nutmeg, to garnish

Add all the ingredients into a mixing glass and fill with ice. Cap with a Boston shaker and shake vigorously. Strain into a chilled glass. Garnish with a little grated nutmeg.

HOT TODDY

Originally a hot drink dating back to early Victorian times, made with sweetened alcohol, water and various spices. Said to be a sure cure for the common cold, drink enough of these and they'll cure almost anything!

Glass: latte glass

Method: build and stir

Recipe

2 oz Scotch whisky

½ oz honey syrup

1 oz lemon juice

1 cracked cinnamon stick

4 cloves

Grated nutmeg

Dash of Angostura bitters

Hot water

Place all the ingredients in a latte glass and top with hot water.

VARIATION

A winter favourite is mulled wine, which uses red wine instead of whisky and spices such as liquorice, cardamom and ginger, generally with an additional liqueur. The whisky can also be substituted for cognac, rum or amaretto.

TIKI DRINKS

Tiki drinks originated during the 1930s and came about from the restaurants of the day set up by the godfathers of Tiki drinks, Don the Beach and Trader Vic. Tiki drinks generally use tropical flavours and ingredients and their names are influenced by Polynesian and Hawaiian styles. These cocktails should be served in coconuts or hollowed out pineapples and using outlandish garnishes is the order of the day.

PIÑA COLADA

The most famous of the coladas is the Piña Colada, its Spanish translation meaning 'strained pineapple'. The origins of this popular modern classic are found in Puerto Rico in the 1950s–60s, although an earlier version of this recipe, a Piña Fria, was mentioned in the Washington Post in 1906, and was described as a refreshment made from the juice of the pineapple.

Glass: hollowed-out pineapple or 12 oz hurricane

Method: shake & fine-strain

Recipe

1½ oz aged rum

½ oz coconut rum

3 oz pineapple juice or 2 oz fresh pineapple purée

½ oz Coco Lopez coconut cream

½ oz double cream

5 ml sugar syrup (not in the classic version but helps to lift the sweet flavours used)

Ice cubes

Pineapple leaf, to garnish

Add all the ingredients into a mixing glass and fill with ice. Cap with a Boston shaker then shake vigorously. Strain into an ice-filled hollowed-out pineapple or a hurricane glass. Garnish with a pineapple leaf.

MAI TAI (TRADER VIC'S)

'Trader' Vic Bergeron claims to have created this drink for two friends in 1944 at his bar in Oakland, California. The couple had just returned from Tahiti and when they sipped the drink they exclaimed 'Mai Tai Roa Ae' meaning 'out of this world, the best' in Tahitian. Trader Vic's rival, Don the Beachcomber, also claimed to have created it first in 1933, however, we'll leave this one to the Tiki rivalry. The original recipe calls for 17-year-Old J. Wray & Nephew Jamaican rum which is extremely rare so the modern version has also been listed.

MAI TAI (VIC BERGERON'S VERSION)

Glass: 10 oz rocks

Method: shake & strain

Recipe

2 cups of crushed ice

1 large lime

2 oz 17 Year Old J. Wray & Nephew Jamaican rum

½ oz French Garnier orgeat (almond) syrup

½ oz Holland DeKuyper orange curaçao

¼ oz sugar syrup

Cracked ice

Mint sprig, pineapple and maraschino cherry, to garnish

Add all the ingredients into a mixing glass and fill with ice. Cap with a Boston shaker and shake vigorously. Strain into an ice-filled glass. Garnish with a sprig of mint, pineapple and cherry.

MAI TAI (MODERN VERSION)

Glass: 12 oz Collins or Tiki mug

Method: shake & strain

Recipe

1 oz aged rum

½ oz triple sec

¼ oz lime juice

1½ oz pineapple juice

1½ oz orange juice

Dash of grenadine

Ice cubes

½ oz dark rum

Maraschino cherry, to garnish

Add all but the dark rum into a mixing glass and fill with ice. Cap with a Boston shaker and shake. Strain into a glass and top with the dark rum. Garnish with a cherry.

PLANTER'S PUNCH

This classic recipe was credited at the turn of the 1900s by Myer's Jamaican Rum founder Fred L Myers and is still written on the back of every bottle. To this day, in the Caribbean and elsewhere, the recipe remains the same. A fifth ingredient has been added over time, which is spice, usually nutmeg, and occasionally bitters.

Glass: 12 oz Collins or Tiki mug

Method: shake & strain

Recipe

½ oz demerara sugar syrup

1 oz lime juice

1½ oz aged rum (Myer's Jamaican Rum)

2 oz chilled water (this can be replaced by using fresh pineapple and/or orange juice)

Ice cubes

Mint sprig, lime wedge and an orange slice, to garnish

Add all the ingredients to a mixing glass and fill with ice. Cap with a Boston shaker and shake vigorously. Strain into an ice-filled glass. Garnish with a sprig of mint, lime wedge and an orange slice. The following rhyme helps bartenders remember the recipe for a punch:
One part sweet (sugar)
Two parts sour (lime juice)
Three parts strong (alcohol, generally rum)
Four parts weak (water)

ZOMBIE

This one was invented by the infamous Ernest Raymond Beaumont-Gannt (aka Don the Beachcomber) in the late 1930s and is a lethal blend of rums.

Glass: 12 oz Collins, Tiki mug or hurricane glass

Method: shake & strain

Recipe

1 oz light rum

1 oz aged rum

½ oz orgeat syrup

½ oz triple sec

½ oz lemon juice

½ oz sugar syrup

2 oz orange juice

Ice cubes

½ oz Bacardi 151 rum

Orange slice, maraschino cherry, lime wedge, pineapple leaf and mint sprig, to garnish

Add the first seven ingredients into a mixing glass and fill with ice. Cap with a Boston shaker and shake vigorously. Strain into an ice-filled glass or Tiki mug. The 151 rum can either be drizzled over the top or set alight first then poured over the drink. Take extreme precaution when handling fire.

NON-ALCOHOLIC COCKTAILS

Virgin cocktails, mocktails, or simply non-alcoholic cocktails – call them what you will – this selection offers an interesting range of mixed drinks, minus the liquor. Try experimenting with juices, cordials, syrups, purées, fresh fruits and herbs to create your own mocktails.

HOMEMADE LEMONADE

My Welsh aunty used to make batches of this stuff! The only way to make this is with fresh lemons and there is no substitute. The recipe can be adapted to suit a sweet or sour palate.

Method: shake & fine-strain

Glass: 12 oz Collins

Recipe

1 oz lemon juice

½ oz sugar syrup (adjust to taste)

Ice cubes

Soda water

Lemon wedge, to garnish

Add the lemon juice and sugar syrup into a mixing glass add fill with ice. Cap with a Boston shaker and shake vigorously. Strain into an ice-filled glass. Top with soda and garnish with a wedge of lemon.

VARIATIONS

There are literally hundreds of flavoured lemonades that can be made using berry and fruit syrups in place of regular sugar syrup. Replace sugar syrup with cherry syrup to make a Cherryade, raspberry syrup to make a Raspberryade, or grenadine to make a Pink Lemonade. The soda can also be substituted here for cola to make an Ice Tea.

ELDERFLOWER AND MINT LEMONADE

Glass: 12 oz Collins or Hurricane

Method: shake & fine-strain

Recipe

6–8 mint leaves

1 oz lemon juice

½ oz elderflower cordial

5 ml sugar syrup

Ice cubes

Soda water

Lemon wedge or slice and mint sprig, to garnish

Add the first four ingredients into a mixing glass and fill with ice. Cap with a Boston shaker and shake vigorously. Strain into an ice-filled glass. Top with soda and garnish with a wedge or slice of lemon and a sprig of mint.

*MINTED APPLEBERRY

A perfect spring and summer cooler combining fresh berry flavours with mint and apple. Ensure you shake this well to combine all the flavours. Spirits such as gin, vodka, rum, bourbon and Scotch whisky work well as a base for an alcoholic version of this drink.

Glass: 12 oz Collins

Method: shake & fine-strain

Recipe

6–8 fresh raspberries or 1 oz raspberry purée

6–8 mint leaves

1 oz cranberry juice

2 oz apple juice

Ice cubes

Lemonade

Raspberry and mint sprig, to garnish

Add the first four ingredients into a mixing glass and fill with ice. Cap with a Boston shaker and shake vigorously. Strain into an ice-filled glass. Top with lemonade and garnish with a raspberry and a sprig of mint.

CHERRY BAKEWELL

A simple combination of syrups creates a drink that tastes just like Mr Kipling's Cherry Bakewell tarts, and children love this drink as much as adults!

Glass: 12 oz Collins

Method: shake & strain

Recipe

½ oz orgeat syrup

½ oz cherry syrup

2 oz cranberry juice

Ice cubes

Lemonade

Maraschino cherry and lemon slice, to garnish

Add the syrups and cranberry juice into a mixing glass and fill with ice. Cap with a Boston shaker and shake vigorously. Strain into an ice-filled glass. Top with lemonade and garnish with a cherry and a slice of lemon.

VIRGIN MULE

A simple non-alcoholic version of the Moscow Mule.

Method: shake & strain

Glass: 12 oz Collins

Recipe

1 oz lime juice

½ oz sugar syrup

Ice cubes

Ginger beer

Lime wedge, to garnish

Add the lime juice and sugar syrup into a mixing glass and fill with ice. Cap with a Boston shaker and shake vigorously. Strain into an ice-filled glass. Top with ginger beer and garnish with a wedge of lime.

POUSSE-CAFÉS

Translates literally from the French as 'pushes coffee', this layered drink makes a perfect after-dinner cocktail to have with or after coffee. It was introduced in New Orleans in the 1840s and became quite popular throughout the US by the turn of the century. Each layer is meant to complement the next and should be sipped slowly to savour each flavour. Not all brands of liqueur will have the same density or weight. Always pour the heaviest liqueur first and proceed with the next heaviest, ending with the lightest.

B52

The most popular of shooters and, the B52 is a great drink to sip on after dinner. There are a number of variations which replace the Cointreau. Use Galliano for a B57 and vodka for a B53.

Glass: 2 oz shot glass
Method: layer
Recipe
½ oz Coffee liqueur
½ oz Baileys Irish Cream
½ oz Cointreau

Layer each liqueur/spirit in the order listed above. Finish by setting fire to the Cointreau. The Cointreau can also be set on fire in a brandy balloon then poured into the drink (see page 101 for full instructions and safety precautions for handling fire).

JAM DOUGHNUT

This drink really does taste like a raspberry-filled doughnut coated in sugar. Try using other berry liqueurs in place of Chambord, such as Crème de Mure (blackberry), Crème de Cassis (blackcurrant) or Crème de Fraise (strawberry).

Glass: 1 oz shot glass
Method: layer
Recipe
Sugar syrup
Granulated white sugar
¼ oz Chambord or raspberry liqueur
½ oz Baileys Irish Cream

Sugar rim the shot glass by dipping it in the sugar syrup, then in the granulated sugar. Layer each spirit in the order listed.

BRAIN HAEMORRHAGE

Other names that have been given to this rather unattractive looking drink include, Monkey's Brain. Although this drink looks ugly, it has a surprisingly sweet taste.

Glass: 1 oz shot glass
Method: build
Recipe
½ oz peach schnapps
¼ oz Baileys Irish Cream
Dash of Grenadine

Pour the peach schnapps into a shot glass. Slowly pour the Baileys then the grenadine into the centre of the liquid.

ACKNOWLEDGEMENTS/INDEX

My mother introduced me to this industry very early on, both through her love of running pubs and pure graft, to give my brother and I a better life. Her influence and hard work have been an inspiration throughout my career and I love her dearly. My big bro Andy is responsible for continuing my passion for this industry by introducing me to my very first bar job and to every bar owner he met in Europe. Thank you for the opportunities this presented me with.

Big love to my friends and family who have tolerated my incessant obsession with cocktails and bartending since I was a teenager, you know who you are. The bartenders and work colleagues I have trained and met around the world who have listened to my ramblings of bartending and cocktails and who have equally inspired me to take my craft to that next level.

Anil Sabharwal, a friend since the beginning of Shaker BarSchools and a true ambassador for professional bartending. Myles Cunliffe, you, my friend, have been and always will be my definition of the consummate professional bartender and your help with pulling the photography together for this book was truly appreciated.

And finally this book is dedicated to my fiancée Tree; without her I would not have been able to realise my ambitions. Your support and dedication have been amazing.

The publishers would like to thank Chris and Antoine at the Puzzle Pub on Gray's Inn Road, London, for their help with the shoot.

INDEX

Page numbers in **bold** refer to a cocktail recipe.

A
absinthe 85, 86; Friends 106
after dinner drinks 150–155
Aftershock 86
Agavero 86
Alize 85
Amaretto 85
Amer Picon 83
Americano 82, **126**, 127
Aperol 83
Atlantic Ice Tea 122
Autumn/Winter Breeze 116

B
B52 **156**
Bacardi Cocktail **135**
Basil Grande **142**

beer 28, 40, 42, 70, 91–93
Bellini 39
Benedictine 54, 86, 127
Between the Sheets **136**
Beverly Hills Ice Tea 122
bitters 83, 105
Black Russian **150**
Bloody: Caesar 117; Maria 117; Mary 50, 58, **117**; Mary Buffet 117; Mary-Lou 117; Med 117
Blue Blazer 6
Blue Hawaiian 38
Bombeirinho 75
bourbon 69, 70, 104, 105, 112
Brain Haemorrhage **157**
Bramble 63, **131**
brandy 39, 72, 79–81, 104; Alexander 81, **150**; apricot 85; Armagnac 79, 81; Buck 81; Crusta 81; cherry 79, 85; Cognac 79–81; Flip 81; Grand Marnier 85; grappa 79; Julep 81; Slivovitz 79
Bubbling Berries 39

C
cachaça 75, 105
Caipirinha 30, 75, 105, **124**; Fruit **125**; Watermelon 105
Caipiriskey 125
Caipirisky 105, 125
Caipirissima 105, 125
Caipirosca 37, 105, 125
Campari 83
Camparina 125
Camperinha 105
Canadian 110
Cape Cod 60, **115**, 116
Caribbean Breeze 116
Chambord 85
Champagne 39, 88; cocktails 39, 75, 148–149, **149**
Chartreuse 54, 86, 127
Cherry: Bakewell **155**; Heering 85
Clement Shrubb 85
cocktails 6, 9, 98, 104–105, 106, 109, 114–118; classics 118–128; non-alcoholic 154–155; recipes

108–157
Cointreau 51, 78, 85
Collins 105, 120–122; Brandy
    (Pierre) 81, 119; Colonel 119;
    Cucumber **120**; Elderflower 105,
    121; Jack 119; Jerry **120**; John
    118; Jose 119; Michael 119;
    Peach 105; Pedro 119; Sandy/Jock
    119; Tom 63, **118**
Cosmopolitan 44, 115, **141**
Crème de… liqueurs 85, 86
Cuarenta Y Tres 85
Cuba Libre 74, **112**
Cuban Mule 105, 133
Curaçao 85

D
Daiquiri 37, 38, 74 , 99; Bacardi
    Cocktail **135**; Between the Sheets
    136; Cachaça 75; Classic **134**;
    Fruit **135**; 137; Raspberry 105;
    Sidecar **136**; strawberry 41;
    Strawberry and Balsamic 105, **134**;
    Vanilla 105; Vanilla/Cinnamon/
    Caramel/Honey **135**
Dark 'n' Stormy 110, 112
Dean Martin 140
Distinctively Botanical **143**
Drambuie 86

F
Fernet Branca 83
Fizz: Gin 73; Golden 118; Ramos
    132; Silver 118
Flaming B52 39
Frangelico 85
Freddie Fudpucker 114
French 39, 75

G
Galliano 86
garnishes 21, 41–51, 109, 140, 141

Gibson Martini 50, 140
Gimlet 63
gin 59, 61–63, 104, 105; and Tonic
    61, 63, **111**; Fix 63; Rickey **111**,
    112
glasses/glassware 21, 28, 36,
    37–40, 51, 108, 107, 110
Glayva 86
Grand Marnier 85
Greyhound 116

H
Harvard 145
Harvey Wallbanger **114**
Hierbas 86
highballs 110–113
Homemade Lemonade **154**
Horse's Neck **110**
Hot Toddy **151**

I
Illy Coffee Liqueur 86
Irish coffee 40

J
Jägermeister 83, 86, 127
Jam Doughnut **157**
Japanese Slipper 137

K
Kahlúa 86
Kentucky Ice Tea 122
Ketel One 59
Kir Royal 38
Krupkin 86
Kwai Feh 85

L
Limoncello 85
liqueurs 84–86, 104, 106
Long Beach Ice Tea 122
Long Island Ice Tea **122**

M
Madeira 82
Mai Tai 74, **152**
Malibu 85
Mandarine Napoléon 85
Manhattan 67, 70, 82, 99,
    145–147; Harvard 147; Perfect **149**;
    Rob Roy 68, 147, 149; Shaken
    148; Star Cocktail 147; Stirred **148**;
    Thyme for Johnnie **149**
Maraschino 85
Margarita 37, 38, 51, 78, **137**;
    modifier theory 105; Passion Fruit
    105, **137**; Pineapple and Black
    Pepper 105, **138**; My Mexican
    Honey 105, **138**; Vanilla 51
Martinez Cocktail **139**
Martini 38, 61, 63, 99, **139**,
    139–144; Basil Grande **142**; Bone
    Dry or Extra Extra Dry 140;
    Breakfast **142**; Cosmopolitan 44,
    115, **141**; Cucumber 50, **143**;
    Dean Martin 140; Dickens 140;
    Distinctively Botanical 143;
    Espresso **144**; Extra Dry 140;
    Filthy 140; flavoured 140;
    Franklin 140; French **144**;
    fresh fruit 140; Fruit Cosmos 141;
    Gibson 50, 140; Lychee 48;
    Marmalade 142; Martinez Cocktail
    139; Metropolitan 141; modified
    variations 140; Naked 140;
    Pass the Dutchie **144**; Perfect 140;
    Purple Cosmo 141; Saketini 140;
    Slightly Wet 140; Sweet 140;
    Vesper 140; Vodka 44, 60;
    White Cosmo 141; Woo Woo 115,
    141; Zhivago 106
Mediterranean Breeze 116
Metropolitan 141
mezcal 76
Midori 85

Mint Julep 70, **125**
Minted Appleberry **155**
Mojito 30, 74, 75, **126**
Mules 132–133; Cuban 105, 133; French 133; Fruit 133; Irish 133; Jägermeister **133**; Jamaican 133; Kentucky 105, 133; London/Chelsea 105, 133; Mexican 105, 133; Moscow 58, 105, **132**; Raspberry **133**; Scottish 105, 133; Tennessee 133; Tuscan 133; Virgin **155**
My Mexican Honey 105, **138**

N
Negroni 82, **127**

O
Old Fashioned 37, 67, 70, 105, **123**; Añejo 74, 78, 105, 123; Brandy 81, 123; Cachaça (Brazilian) 123; Cognac 105; Talisker Re-fashioned **124**; Velho 75; Whisky 105, 123
Opal Nera 86
Orgasm 150
Oriental Breeze 116
Ouzo 86

P
Pass the Dutchie **144**
Passion Fruit Margarita 105, **137**
Passoã 85
Pastis 86
Patron XO 86
Pernod 86
Pimm's 38, 85, **113**
Piña Colada 38, 74, **151**
Pineapple and Black Pepper Margarita 105, **138**
Pisang Ambom 85
Planter's Punch **153**
port 40, 82

Pousse-cafés 155–156
Presbyterian 110
Prosecco 148

R
Red Snapper 63, 117
Rob Roy 68, 147, 149
Ron Miel Canario 86
Rossini 149
rum 71–74, 104, 105; Rickey 112
Russians 37; Russian Spring Punch 38; Toasted White/Black Russian 150

S
Sailor Jerry and cola 112
Salty Dog 116
Sambuca 86
Sangrita **118**
Sazerac 37, 70, **127**
Schnapps 106; peach 85
Screwdriver 58, 60, **114**
Sea Breeze 115, **116**
Sex on the Beach 115, 116
sherry 82
Sidecar **136**
Slings: Brandy 81; Gin 63; Singapore **128**; Strait **128**
Sours 37, 70, 129–132; Amaretto 129, **130**; Amaretto Stone 129; Benedictine 129; Bramble **131**; Brandy 81, 129; Cachaça 129; Drambuie 129; Gin 129; Grapefruit and Honey **131**; Honey Berry **130**; Midori 129, **129**; Pisco 129; Rum 129; Scotch 68, 129; Tuscan 129; Whiskey **129**
Southern Comfort 85, 112
Spiced Ice Tea 122
Star cocktail 147
Strawberry and Balsamic Daiquiri 105
Strega 86

Summer/Bay Breeze 116

T
Talisker Re-fashioned **124**
Tennessee Ice Tea 122
Tequila 32, 76–78, 104, 105, 111, 112; Sunrise **115**
Tetanka 114
Thyme for Johnnie **149**
Tia Maria 86, 112
tiki drinks 74, 151–153
Tokyo Ice Tea 122
Toussaint liqueur 86
Tuaca 86

U
Underberg 83
Unicum 83

V
vermouth 63, 82, 140
vodka 58–60, 104, 105, 111, 112; Rickey 60, **111**

W
Watermelon Caipirinha 105
whisky 58, 64–70, 104; American whiskey 69, 70, 72; Irish whiskey 68–69; Rickey 112
wine 87–90; aromatised/fortified 82, 104
Woo Woo 115, **141**

X
Xante 86

Z
Zombie 38, 47, 74, **153**